REPORT

How Successful Are U.S. Efforts to Build Capacity in Developing Countries?

A Framework to Assess the Global Train and Equip "1206" Program

Jennifer D. P. Moroney, Beth Grill, Joe Hogler, Lianne Kennedy-Boudali, Christopher Paul

Prepared for the Office of the Secretary of Defense

T0308363

NATIONAL DEFENSE RESEARCH INSTITUTE

The research described in this report was prepared for the Office of the Secretary of Defense (OSD). The research was conducted within the RAND National Defense Research Institute, a federally funded research and development center sponsored by OSD, the Joint Staff, the Unified Combatant Commands, the Navy, the Marine Corps, the defense agencies, and the defense Intelligence Community under Contract W74V8H-06-C-0002.

Library of Congress Cataloging-in-Publication Data

How successful are U.S. efforts to build capacity in developing countries? : a framework to assess the Global Train and Equip "1206" Program / Jennifer D. P. Moroney ... [et al.].
     p. cm.
  Includes bibliographical references.
  ISBN 978-0-8330-5310-7 (pbk. : alk. paper)
  1. Security Assistance Program—Evaluation. 2. Military assistance, American—Foreign countries—Evaluation.
3. United States—Armed Forces—Stability operations—Evaluation. 4. Terrorism—Prevention—International cooperation—Evaluation. 5. Combined operations (Military science)—Evaluation. 6. United States—Military relations—Foreign countries. 7. United States—Military policy—Evaluation. I. Moroney, Jennifer D. P., 1973- II. International Security and Defense Policy Center. III. Rand Corporation. IV. United States. Office of the Under Secretary of Defense for Policy. V. Title: Framework to assess the Global Train and Equip "1206" Program.

  UA12.H69 2011
  355'.0320973—dc23

                                                                                                        2011029550

Published 2011 by the RAND Corporation
1776 Main Street, P.O. Box 2138, Santa Monica, CA 90407-2138
1200 South Hayes Street, Arlington, VA 22202-5050
4570 Fifth Avenue, Suite 600, Pittsburgh, PA 15213-2665
RAND URL: http://www.rand.org/
To order RAND documents or to obtain additional information, contact
Distribution Services: Telephone: (310) 451-7002;
Fax: (310) 451-6915; Email: order@rand.org

Preface

The U.S. government has long worked with allies and partners in a security cooperation context, providing various means through which to build their capacities to counter threats. Yet, it is difficult to comprehensively assess how these activities contribute to U.S. objectives. Assessing the effect of security cooperation efforts is extremely important. Security cooperation assessments support informed decisionmaking at the policy, program manager, and execution levels, and they provide stakeholders with the necessary tools to determine which aspects of these investments are most productive and which areas require refinement. This report provides a framework for thinking about, planning for, and implementing security cooperation assessments for the Global Train and Equip "1206" Program, managed by the Office of the Under Secretary of Defense for Policy. The program has its origins in Section 1206 of the National Defense Authorization Act for Fiscal Year 2006, which authorizes the Secretary of Defense, with the concurrence of the Secretary of State, to spend up to $350 million each year to train and equip foreign military and nonmilitary maritime forces to conduct counterterrorism operations and to build the capacity of a foreign nation's military forces to enable it to participate in or support military and stability operations in which U.S. armed forces are involved.

This report documents research performed between July 2010 and January 2011 for a study titled "Identifying Resources to Implement an Assessment Framework for the Global Train and Equip '1206' Program." The findings should be of interest to agencies and to individuals and offices in the U.S. Department of Defense and U.S. Department of State with roles in guiding and overseeing international security cooperation programs and activities, as well as to those who are directly involved with the planning and implementation of these efforts.

This research was sponsored by the Office of the Under Secretary of Defense for Policy and conducted within the International Security and Defense Policy Center of the RAND National Defense Research Institute, a federally funded research and development center sponsored by the Office of the Secretary of Defense, the Joint Staff, the Unified Combatant Commands, the Navy, the Marine Corps, the defense agencies, and the defense Intelligence Community.

For more information on the International Security and Defense Policy Center, see http://www.rand.org/nsrd/ndri/centers/isdp.html or contact the director (contact information is provided on the web page).

Contents

Preface iii

Figures ix

Tables xi

Summary xiii

Acknowledgments xix

Abbreviations xxi

CHAPTER ONE

Introduction 1

The Global Train and Equip "1206" Program: An Overview 2

The Importance of Assessments 3

Study Objectives and Analytical Approach 4

Organization of This Report 6

CHAPTER TWO

RAND's Assessment Framework 7

What Is Assessment? 7

Why Assess? 7

Challenges to 1206 Program Assessment 8

    Determining Causality 8

    Well-Articulated Intermediate Goals to Inform Decisionmaking 8

    Assessment Capabilities of 1206 Program Stakeholders 9

    Multiplicity of and Differing Priorities of Stakeholders 9

    Security Cooperation Data Tracking Systems Are Not Currently Organized for
        1206 Program Assessment 9

    Delegating Assessment Responsibilities 10

    Expectations and Preconceived Notions of Assessment 10

Levels of Assessment: The Hierarchy of Evaluation 10

    Level 1: Assessment of Need for the Program 11

    Level 2: Assessment of Design and Theory 12

    Level 3: Assessment of Process and Implementation 13

    Level 4: Assessment of Outcome and Impact 13

    Level 5: Assessment of Cost-Effectiveness 14

Hierarchy and Nesting 14

Key Insights and the Assessment Framework..15
    Assessment and Objectives..15
    Assessment Roles and Responsibilities 15
    Data Collection and Reporting 17
Conclusion...17

CHAPTER THREE
Exploring the Options for 1206 Program Assessment: Discussions with Key Stakeholders 19
Stakeholder Interviews..19
Stakeholder Perceptions of the 1206 Program...20
    Short Timeline Allows Faster Impact but Creates Administrative Difficulties......................20
    Lack of Funding for Maintenance and Support Creates Concerns About Sustainability...........21
    The Project Design, Selection, Prioritization, and Assessment Processes Are Somewhat
        Unclear 22
    Interagency Cooperation Has Improved, but Data Sharing Is Limited................................22
Stakeholder Observations Relative to Insights of Assessment 23
    Guidance on Assessment Is Needed 23
    Measurable Objectives Are Required on Multiple Levels..24
    1206 Program Assessment Roles and Responsibilities Will Require Clarification....................25
    New Data Collection and Reporting Requirements Are Needed...26
    Improving Coordination with Key Agencies Is Critical...26
Conclusion...26

CHAPTER FOUR
Applying the Framework to the 1206 Program: Results of the Survey.............................27
Survey of 1206 Program Experts...27
    Constructing the Survey..28
    1206 Program Guidance..30
    Survey Respondents 30
Findings and Observations..31
    Formal Guidance on the Assessment Process Is Needed..31
    Measurable Objectives That Explicitly Connect to Broader U.S. Government, Theater,
        Regional, and 1206 Project Goals Are Lacking..32
    Gaps Exist in Data Collection and Reporting Requirements 33
    1206 Program Assessment Roles and Responsibilities Are Currently Unclear.......................36
    Limited Insight into Other DoD Programs May Hinder Cost-Effectiveness Assessments 36
    Respondents Were Not Always Aware of Guidance..37
    Stakeholders Create Their Own Guidance in the Absence of Formal Guidance.....................37
    Assessment Skills Exist but Could Be Improved 37
Conclusions..38

CHAPTER FIVE
Conclusions and Recommendations 39
Findings 40
Recommendations 41
    Recommendation 1: Develop an Implementation Plan for 1206 Program Assessments...........41

Recommendation 2: Develop and Disseminate "Life-Cycle" Guidance for Project Development, Implementation, and Assessment... 41
Recommendation 3: Ensure That 1206 Program Stakeholders Understand Their Assessment Roles.. 41
Recommendation 4: Establish a Process for Setting Objectives at the Project and Activity Levels... 41
Recommendation 5: Systematically Collect Data Regarding Achievement of Objectives and Consider Using Focus Groups to Develop Metrics................................ 42
Recommendation 6: Identify Data Collectors Based on Their Proximity to the Action............ 42
Recommendation 7: Host an Annual Conference of 1206 Program Stakeholders at the Policymaking Level.. 42
Recommendation 8: Consider Developing an Automated Tool to Facilitate the Collection and Reporting of Assessment Data... 42
Recommendation 9: Consider Hiring Outside Support or Appointing Career Staff to Be "Program Representatives" at Each COCOM 43
The Implemention Plan 43
Track 1: Near-Term Actions 43
Track 2: Long-Term Actions... 45
Rollout of the Assessment Implementation Plan... 46
Conclusion... 46

APPENDIXES
A. **The Assessment Survey** 47
B. **Focused Discussions**... 65

Bibliography... 67

Figures

S.1. Five Levels: The Assessment Hierarchy.. xv
S.2. Track 1 of the Assessment Implementation Plan... xvii
S.3. Track 2 of the Assessment Implementation Plan.. xviii
S.4. Proposed Rollout for the Assessment Implementation Plan xviii
1.1. Five Levels: The Assessment Hierarchy.. 5
4.1. Data Sources Identified for Process and Implementation Assessments..................... 35
4.2. Data Sources Identified for Outcome Assessments 35

Tables

4.1. Types of 1206 Program Data That Can Be Collected, by Topic............................29
4.2. Disconnects Between Setting Objectives and Program Design.............................32
4.3. Disconnects Between Setting Objectives and Collecting Data on Their Achievement...32
4.4. Types of Assessment Data Collected by Survey Respondents...............................33

Summary

The U.S. government has long worked with allies and partners to build their capacities to counter threats through various means, including training, equipping, and exercising, as well as through relationship-building activities such as workshops and conferences, staff talks, and education. Yet, it is challenging to comprehensively assess exactly how these activities have contributed to U.S. objectives. Security cooperation activities are long-term and geographically dispersed, and there is currently no comprehensive framework for assessing these programs.

Assessing the impact of security cooperation efforts is inherently difficult but extremely important. In short, security cooperation assessments support informed decisionmaking at the policy, program manager, and execution levels, and they provide stakeholders at all levels of government with effective tools to determine which aspects of these investments are most productive and which areas require refinement.

Those who plan and execute security cooperation efforts intuitively know whether their individual programs have successfully gained ground with their respective partner nations. At the most basic level, officials assert that the U.S.–partner nation relationship is simply "better" than it was prior to executing the activity. These assertions are difficult to validate empirically, however.

At present, assessments of security cooperation programs, if they are done at all, are largely conducted by the same organizations that executed the activities. Thus, these assessments, no matter how carefully carried out, are subject to concerns about bias on the part of the assessors. Objective assessments, when available, provide valuable data on which meaningful discussions about program funding can be grounded.

This report provides a framework for thinking about, planning for, and implementing security cooperation assessments for the 1206 Program managed by Office of the Under Secretary of Defense for Policy (OUSD[P]). It argues that such assessments provide the necessary justification for continuing, expanding, altering, or cutting back on existing programs. Without insight into the successes and weaknesses of security cooperation programs, it is impossible to make informed decisions about how best to allocate the resources available for their use.

The Global Train and Equip "1206" Program

The National Defense Authorization Act for Fiscal Year 2006 established the authority for the 1206 Program. Section 1206 of that legislation authorizes the Secretary of Defense, with the concurrence of the Secretary of State, to spend up to $350 million each year to train and equip foreign military and nonmilitary maritime forces to conduct counterterrorism opera-

xiv   How Successful Are U.S. Efforts to Build Capacity in Developing Countries?

tions and to enable the foreign partner to participate in or support military and stability operations in which U.S. armed forces are involved. This authority is set to expire at the end of fiscal year 2011, but Congress may renew Section 1206, as it has in the past.

The 1206 Program enables the U.S. Department of Defense (DoD) to conduct capacity-building activities focused on counterterrorism and stability operations with foreign military partners. By law, Section 1206 authority has two discrete uses:

- to build the capacity of a foreign country's national military forces to enable that country to conduct counterterrorism operations or participate in or support military and stability operations in which U.S. armed forces are involved
- to build the capacity of a foreign country's maritime security forces to conduct counterterrorism operations.

Study Approach

RAND was asked by the Office of the Assistant Secretary of Defense for Special Operations/Low-Intensity Conflict and Interdependent Capabilities (OASD[SO/LIC&IC]) in OUSD(P) for assistance in identifying key stakeholders, their roles, and sources of data in support of a comprehensive assessment of the 1206 Program. RAND was also asked to develop the key elements of an implementation plan that would allow the repeated assessment of the program's outcomes and cost-effectiveness.

The RAND study team adopted a multistep approach to achieving these study objectives. We first focused on identifying current roles, data sources, and ongoing assessment processes through a series of discussions with key policymakers, legislators, and project implementers in the field. We then developed and deployed a survey designed to gather information on the roles, processes, and responsibilities of stakeholder organizations in the 1206 Program, as well as to elicit information regarding assessment guidance and skills. Next, we analyzed the survey results to determine which stakeholders were best suited for the collection of data in support of 1206 Program assessments and which stakeholders could potentially conduct such assessments. We then combined our findings from the survey analysis and the interviews and presented them to the sponsor. Based on the survey findings, we developed recommendations and key elements of an assessment implementation plan.

This report lays the groundwork for a comprehensive assessment of the 1206 Program rather than for various "snapshot-in-time" assessments of specific 1206 projects around the world. It takes a longer-term view, with the understanding that accurate assessments, especially those focused on outcomes and cost-effectiveness, require time and effort.

Assessment Framework

We based our analysis of the 1206 Program on five assessment levels:

- Level 1: need for the program
- Level 2: design and theory
- Level 3: process and implementation

- Level 4: outcome and impact
- Level 5: cost-effectiveness (relative to other, similar programs).[1]

We think of these five levels, integral to the assessment framework, as a hierarchy, depicted graphically in Figure S.1.

In this hierarchy, a positive assessment at a higher level relies on positive assessments at the lower levels. By "positive," we mean that the assessment reveals that associated objectives are being met. Accordingly, problems at a higher level of the hierarchy link to problems at lower levels of the hierarchy. For example, if a cost-effectiveness assessment reveals a problem, one can examine information from the lower levels of the hierarchy to fully understand the root cause of that problem.

Interviews and Survey Approach and Findings

Chapters Three and Four discuss the approach and findings from our research effort, which included 14 interviews with 1206 Program stakeholders in DoD and the U.S. Department of State (DoS) and staff from key congressional committees. Interview questions helped the team identify current roles in the 1206 Program, as well as data sources and existing assessment processes for the program.

We also conducted an online survey of stakeholder representatives to gain specific insights into current and potential assessment capabilities. Fifty-six of the 136 individuals asked to take the survey responded, which is approximately 40 percent. Survey questions were grouped

Figure S.1
Five Levels: The Assessment Hierarchy

Level 5	Assessment of cost-effectiveness
Level 4	Assessment of outcome/impact
Level 3	Assessment of process and implementation
Level 2	Assessment of design and theory
Level 1	Assessment of need for the program

SOURCE: Adapted from Peter H. Rossi, Mark W. Lipsey, and Howard E. Freeman, *Evaluation: A Systematic Approach,* 7th ed., Thousand Oaks, Calif.: Sage Publications, 2004, Exhibit 3-C. Used with permission.

NOTE: For a detailed discussion of the assessment hierarchy, see Christopher Paul, Harry J. Thie, Elaine Reardon, Deanna Weber Prine, and Laurence Smallman, *Implementing and Evaluating an Innovative Approach to Simulation Training Acquisition,* Santa Monica, Calif.: RAND Corporation, MG-442-OSD, 2006.
RAND *TR1121-S.1*

---

[1]   The study did not include a cost-effectiveness assessment, which is a measure of relative benefit based on cost and requires comparison with similar programs. We did not have access to the required budgetary information to carry out such an analysis.

into four broad areas derived from the assessment hierarchy presented in Figure S.1: process implementation, process design and development, program recommendations, and program decisions. The team was able to connect each respondent's answers to possible assessment roles.

The interviews and survey results clearly indicate that the 1206 Program stakeholder community is in favor of instituting an assessment framework. Such a framework should include specific guidance on assessments, measureable objectives at the project level (in particular), and data collection and data reporting processes. It is clear from the results that much data are currently being collected, but they are not reaching policymakers in a systematic way. Interview participants also mentioned the need to improve coordination between DoD and DoS at all levels.

Key Findings, Recommendations, and the Assessment Implementation Plan

This report offers five key findings and nine recommendations, as well as some thoughts on an assessment implementation plan.

Findings

Our analysis of the survey data revealed the following key findings:

- There is a lack of formal guidance on the assessment process for the 1206 Program. Such guidance would help ensure that all 1206 stakeholders understand the importance of assessing the program in a comprehensive way.
- Measurable objectives that explicitly connect to broader U.S. government, theater, regional, and 1206 Program goals are currently lacking for the 1206 Program.
- Gaps seem to exist in the data collection and reporting requirements process. Data are not reaching stakeholders charged with conducting assessments.
- Assessment roles and responsibilities for 1206 Program stakeholders are currently unclear and unassigned.
- Coordination among key stakeholders, in both DoD and other agencies—namely, DoS and key congressional committees—could be improved.

Recommendations

Our analysis of the survey data resulted in the following recommendations:

- Develop an implementation plan for 1206 Program assessments.
- Develop and disseminate "life-cycle" guidance for project development, implementation, and assessment.
- Ensure that 1206 Program stakeholders understand their assessment roles.
- Establish a process for setting objectives at the project and activity levels.
- Systematically collect data on the achievement of objectives. Consider using focus groups to develop metrics.
- Identify data collectors based on their proximity to the action.
- Host an annual conference of 1206 Program stakeholders at the policymaking level.

- Consider developing an automated tool to facilitate the collection and reporting of assessment data.
- Consider hiring outside support or appointing career staff members to be "program representatives" for the 1206 Program at each of the respective combatant commands (COCOMs).

Assessment Implementation Plan

Our assessment implementation plan is divided into two tracks (near-term actions and longer-term actions), but several of the activities can be undertaken simultaneously as resources and timing allow. Track 1, near-term actions, detailed in Figure S.2, offers relatively low-cost steps that can be implemented in the short term.

In contrast, track 2 comprises some longer-term, potentially more costly and time-consuming steps, as shown in Figure S.3.

A proposed rollout plan is presented in Figure S.4. The rollout plan provides notional timelines for instituting track 1 and track 2 of the assessment implementation plan.

Phase 1 of the rollout focuses on internal changes within OUSD(P) that can be accomplished relatively quickly. Phase 2 involves other stakeholders in DoD and DoS and outreach to key congressional committees; it centers on a key meeting with senior representatives from stakeholder organizations. Phase 3 of the rollout involves the execution of the implementation plan.

Figure S.2
Track 1 of the Assessment Implementation Plan

1. Provide formal guidance on assessment
– Identify sources of objectives and who sets those objectives
– Describe the assessment process, step-by-step
– Identify timelines for conducting assessments

2. Establish 1206 assessment roles and responsibilities
– Identify specific roles within the program
– Consider specialized training
– Obtain partner-nation input and feedback

3. Set data collection and reporting requirements
– Identify specific offices responsible for collecting certain types of data, based on functions currently performed
– Ensure that stakeholders know which data to collect
– Establish routine reporting requirements with standardized formats and timelines
– Avoid redundancy, unnecessary data collection, etc., recognizing that this is an "additional duty"

4. Improve coordination with key agencies
– Seek input from all stakeholders early on
  • Internal: OUSD(P), DSCA, services, COCOMs
  • External: DoS, congressional staffs, partner nations

NOTE: DSCA = Defense Security Cooperation Agency.
RAND *TR1121-S.2*

Figure S.3
Track 2 of the Assessment Implementation Plan

1. Set measurable objectives that explicitly connect to broader U.S. government, theater, regional, and 1206 Program goals
– Consider both the overall program level and the project level
– Explicitly connect the projects to counterterrorism or building partnership capacity goals or both
  • Ensure connections to higher-level 1206 Program guidance
– Define the process for setting objectives
  • Consider drawing from the U.S. Pacific Command model
– Ensure that objectives are clearly measurable
  • Focus on the longer-term outcomes that cannot be measured in one year

2. Refine roles for data collection and analysis based on track 1 lessons
– Institute a consistent but flexible process

3. Implement an automated system for data collection and assessment—follow-on from current RAND study (the survey instrument)
– Identify potential "off-the-shelf" automated tools
  • Automated tool should be "modular" to include results of multiple projects
– Consider asking the Office of the Deputy Assistant Secretary of Defense for Partnership Strategy and Stability Operations to develop such an automated tool
– Conduct a pilot test of the automated data collection tool

RAND TR1121-S.3

Figure S.4
Proposed Rollout for the Assessment Implementation Plan

Phase 1: Office of the Secretary of Defense internal (1–6 months)
– Consolidate existing guidance, prepare assessment implementation plan
– Issue assessment implementation plan
  • Define process for setting measureable objectives and data collection, assign initial roles and responsibilities at HQ and in the field (COCOMs)
– Begin development of automated data collection tool
  • Perhaps with the support of a new assessment office in the Office of the Deputy Assistant Secretary of Defense for Partnership Strategy and Stability Operations

Phase 3: Implementation (12+ months)
– Begin execution of assessment implementation plan

Phase 2: Involve other stakeholders (6–12 months)
– Hold a strategic-level meeting, to include OUSD(P), DSCA, DoS, COCOM J4 (logistics)/J5 (strategic plans and policy)/J8 (force structure, resources, and assessment), and the services at the GS-15/colonel level, on 1206 to complement the execution-level meetings run by DSCA
  • Socialize assessment concept, coordinate guidance, solicit feedback
  • Identify strategic-level assessment process for 1206 (cost-effectiveness level)
– Share assessment implementation plan with key congressional committees
– Confirm and finalize assigned stakeholder roles
– Refine automated tool

RAND TR1121-S.4

Acknowledgments

The authors are grateful for the support of many individuals over the course of this study effort. First, we would like to express our sincere thanks for the terrific support from our study sponsors in OASD(SO/LIC&IC), specifically Christel Fonzo-Eberhard, Shannon Culbertson, LTC John Gossart, and Ashley Pixton. We also thank the officials at DSCA, the COCOMs, service headquarters, and DoS and the senior congressional staffers who provided valuable insights that greatly improved the content of this report.

The study team also benefited from the thoughtful and careful reviews provided by Alan Stolberg at the Army War College and Michael Shurkin at RAND. Finally, we thank Michael Neumann for his structural feedback and Melissa McNulty and Cassandra Tate for their administrative support. Any errors are solely the responsibility of the authors.

Abbreviations

AOR	area of responsibility
COCOM	combatant command
DoD	U.S. Department of Defense
DoDI	U.S. Department of Defense instruction
DoS	U.S. Department of State
DSCA	Defense Security Cooperation Agency
FAA	Foreign Assistance Act
FMS	Foreign Military Sales
GAO	U.S. Government Accountability Office
GEF	Guidance for the Employment of the Force
IPR	interim progress review
J5	U.S. Joint Chiefs of Staff Office of Strategic Plans and Policy
NDAA	National Defense Authorization Act
OASD(SO/LIC&IC)	Office of the Assistant Secretary of Defense for Special Operations/Low-Intensity Conflict and Interdependent Capabilities
OSD	Office of the Secretary of Defense
OUSD(P)	Office of the Under Secretary of Defense for Policy
TCP	theater campaign plan
USAFRICOM	U.S. Africa Command
USCENTCOM	U.S. Central Command
USEUCOM	U.S. European Command
USPACOM	U.S. Pacific Command
USSOUTHCOM	U.S. Southern Command

CHAPTER ONE

Introduction

The U.S. government has long worked with allies and partners in a security cooperation context to build their capacities to counter a variety of internal and external threats. The security cooperation activities conducted by the U.S. Department of Defense (DoD) range from the very visible (i.e., training, equipping, and exercising with others) to the less obvious, such as workshops and conferences, staff talks, and providing education. Yet, it is challenging to identify how and to what extent these various activities have contributed to U.S. objectives—whether at the national security, department, combatant command (COCOM), or service level. Security cooperation efforts are both long-term and geographically dispersed, and there is currently no comprehensive framework for assessing these efforts.

Security cooperation assessments are important at all levels—policy, program manager, and execution—because assessments *support decisions*. At the highest levels, assessments provide an organization, such as the Office of the Under Secretary of Defense for Policy (OUSD[P]), with a basis for comparing the effectiveness and efficiency of the many programs it manages. Using these comparisons, assessments can offer informed suggestions for how to improve existing programs or initiate new programs in DoD where gaps are identified. At the program level, assessments assist program and resource managers in making decisions about future security cooperation activities—specifically, whether to cut, expand, alter, or continue current program activities based on their impact. At the execution level, assessments provide important insights into how to most effectively implement activities.

The OUSD(P)-managed Global Train and Equip "1206" Program (hereafter referred to as the "1206 Program") is one such security cooperation program that could benefit greatly from a comprehensive assessment approach. In its April 2010 report on the 1206 Program, the U.S. Government Accountability Office (GAO) recommended that DoD

1. establish a monitoring and evaluation system
2. base sustainment funding decisions on the assessment of results
3. estimate sustainment costs and seek funding commitments from partner nations
4. seek guidance from Congress on how to sustain projects.

DoD concurred with these recommendations.[1]

This report focuses primarily on the first recommendation, the establishment of a system to evaluate the results (or effectiveness/impact) of the program using objective performance

---

[1] U.S. Government Accountability Office, *International Security: DoD and State Need to Improve Sustainment Planning and Monitoring and Evaluation for Section 1206 and 1207 Assistance Programs*, Washington, D.C., GAO-10-431, April 15, 2010, p. 1.

measures, monitoring the program's progress in achieving goals, and reporting this progress in annual performance reports. Such a system can assist program managers as they develop initiatives that provide appropriate capabilities and capacities that partner nations are likely to employ, and it can help answer key questions regarding the 1206 Program's effectiveness in developing them. The analysis conducted by the RAND team can also inform the second GAO recommendation, as the framework we have developed includes assessing the results, or rather the impacts made on partner nations through the 1206 Program activities—what we call "outcomes." The latter two GAO recommendations were beyond the scope of this study.

The Global Train and Equip "1206" Program: An Overview

The National Defense Authorization Act (NDAA) for Fiscal Year 2006 established the authority for the 1206 Program. Section 1206 of the NDAA authorizes the Secretary of Defense, with the concurrence of the Secretary of State, to spend up to $350 million each year to train and equip foreign military and nonmilitary maritime forces, including coast guards, to conduct counterterrorist operations or to support military and stability operations in which U.S. armed forces are involved. This authority is set to expire at the end of fiscal year 2011, but Congress may renew Section 1206, as it has in the past.

By law, Section 1206 authority has two discrete uses:

- to build the capacity of a foreign country's national military forces to enable that country to conduct counterterrorism operations or participate in or support military and stability operations in which U.S. armed forces are involved
- to build the capacity of a foreign country's maritime security forces to conduct counterterrorism operations.

A unique characteristic of the 1206 Program is the required coordination between DoD and the U.S. Department of State (DoS). The NDAA regulations established an interagency implementation process. Within DoD, the Office of the Assistant Secretary of Defense for Special Operations/Low-Intensity Conflict and Interdependent Capabilities (OASD[SO/LIC&IC]) is charged with overall responsibility for the 1206 Program. This office coordinates primarily with DoS's Bureau of Political-Military Affairs. All 1206 Program project proposals are considered within this interagency process.

The 1206 Program process includes a number of essential steps. DoD and DoS annually solicit project proposals, which are revised each year in accordance with guidelines and instructions to reflect lessons learned, congressional concerns, and other considerations. The proposal template requires stakeholders, such as country team representatives and COCOM staffs, to include basic assessment information, including how the effectiveness of the project will be measured, the expected time frame for realizing operational impacts, key train and equip milestones, and quantitative and qualitative metrics that will be used to measure the effectiveness of the program. Interagency boards review the proposals, which must be approved by both the relevant U.S. combatant commander and ambassador, and select projects to recommend to the Secretaries of Defense and State for final funding approval. Once projects are fully approved and funded, DoD and DoS, after notifying designated congressional committees, may implement them.[2] For approved projects, the Defense Security Cooperation Agency (DSCA), operating under guidance from OUSD(P), assumes overall responsibility for procuring training and equipment. Security assistance officers posted at U.S. embassies (who report to both the ambassador and the relevant U.S. geographic combatant commands) are then responsible for coordinating in-country project implementation.[3]

As with any other security cooperation program, the 1206 Program has administrative rules and guidance that must be followed by all 1206 Program stakeholders. First, COCOMs and appropriate embassy officials jointly formulate all 1206 Program proposals. Second, 1206 Program funding is subject to restrictions for sanctioned countries and those with known human rights abuses. Third, 1206 Program funding must be obligated by the end of each fiscal year. Fourth, 1206 Program funding does not support Iraqi or Afghan security forces.[4] Fifth, all 1206 Program proposals undergo a legal, political-military feasibility review.[5] For the purposes of this report, it is worth noting that the current guidance on the program does not, however, mention the need to conduct assessments at the project level.

In general, 1206 Program funding should not be used to

1. backfill DoD or DoS shortfalls
2. fund equipment with extraordinarily long production lead times that will not meet near-term military needs
3. fund activities that are, in reality, counternarcotics missions
4. fund programs that must be continued over long periods (more than three years) to achieve—as opposed to sustain—a partner's capability.[6]

Specifically, equipment, supplies, or training may be provided to build the capacity of a foreign country's national military forces to conduct counterterrorist operations or military/stability operations in which the U.S. military is involved.

The Importance of Assessments

Assessing the impact of security cooperation efforts is inherently difficult, but it is important for providing stakeholders at all levels of government with effective tools to determine which aspects of these investments are most productive and which areas require refinement.

Those who plan and execute security cooperation efforts intuitively know whether their individual programs have successfully gained ground with their respective partner nations. At the most basic level, officials assert that the U.S.–partner nation relationship is simply "better" than it was prior to executing the activity.

---

[2] Congressional notification is required not less than 15 days before initiating assistance in any country.

[3] U.S. Government Accountability Office, 2010, p. 8.

[4] Although not expressly addressed in the legislation, it was not the intent of Congress to provide another funding source for Iraqi and Afghan security forces through the 1206 Program authority. However, it is allowable to use 1206 Program funds to train and equip partner nations preparing to deploy to Iraq and Afghanistan in support of U.S. forces.

[5] Discussion with OASD(SO/LIC&IC) officials.

[6] Discussion with OASD(SO/LIC&IC) officials.

Although these assertions appear to ring true, it is difficult to empirically validate such a general sense of accomplishment, especially for senior DoD policymakers and Congress. At present, assessments of security cooperation activities, to the extent that they are done, are largely conducted by the organization that executed the activities. Thus, these assessments, no matter how carefully carried out, are subject to concerns about bias on the part of the assessors. Moreover, self-assessment is even less convincing when conducted by program managers, planners, and executers, who often rotate rapidly, sometimes within the span of a year. Due to the transience of their positions, these individuals do not typically have the experience necessary to understand and evaluate a program's long-term effectiveness in a country. In addition to subject or functional expertise, objectivity and longevity are therefore two important characteristics for participants in the assessment process.

DoD decisionmakers rely on assessments to establish programmatic priorities and determine the allocation of resources. Objective assessments provide valuable data on which to ground meaningful discussions about program funding. As mentioned previously, assessments provide the necessary justification for continuing, expanding, altering, or cutting back on existing programs. Without insight into the current successes and weaknesses of security cooperation programs, it is impossible for DoD officials to make informed decisions about how best to allocate those resources available for their use.

In addition to serving the needs of high-level decisionmakers, assessments provide critical information to those directly involved in the planning and implementation of security cooperation programs. Ultimately, quality assessment of these programs contributes to *improved decisionmaking* at all stages, including oversight, planning, management, resourcing, and execution, and it has the potential to increase both the effectiveness and the efficiency of security cooperation efforts. This report provides a framework for thinking about, planning for, and implementing security cooperation assessments for the 1206 Program managed by OUSD(P).[7]

Study Objectives and Analytical Approach

RAND was asked by OASD(SO/LIC&IC), within OUSD(P), for assistance in identifying key stakeholders, their roles, and sources of data in support of a comprehensive assessment of the 1206 Program. RAND was also asked to develop the key elements of an implementation plan that would allow the repeated assessment of the program's outcomes and cost-effectiveness.

The study included five main tasks. The first involved identifying current roles, data sources, and ongoing assessment processes through a series of discussions with key policymakers, legislators, and project implementers in the field. As part of the second task, the study team developed and deployed a survey designed to gather information on the roles, processes, and responsibilities of stakeholder organizations in the 1206 Program, as well as to elicit information regarding assessment guidance and skills.

---

[7]   See Jennifer D. P. Moroney, Jefferson P. Marquis, Cathryn Quantic Thurston, and Gregory F. Treverton, *A Framework to Assess Programs for Building Partnerships*, Santa Monica, Calif.: RAND Corporation, MG-863-OSD, 2009, pp. 9–10. See also Jennifer D. P. Moroney, Joe Hogler, Jefferson P. Marquis, Christopher Paul, John E. Peters, and Beth Grill, *Developing an Assessment Framework for U.S. Air Force Building Partnerships Programs*, Santa Monica, Calif.: RAND Corporation, MG-868-AF, 2010, and Jefferson P. Marquis, Richard E. Darilek, Jasen J. Castillo, Cathryn Quantic Thurston, Anny Wong, Cynthia Huger, Andrea Mejia, Jennifer D. P. Moroney, Brian Nichiporuk, and Brett Steele, *Assessing the Value of U.S. Army International Activities*, Santa Monica, Calif.: RAND Corporation, MG-329-A, 2006.

The third task involved analyzing the survey results to determine which stakeholders were best suited for the collection of data in support of 1206 Program assessments and which stakeholders could potentially conduct such assessments. The analysis was based on the five levels of the assessment hierarchy:

- Level 1, "need for the program" (or activity), focuses on the problem to be solved or goal to be met and identifies the population to be served and the kinds of services that might contribute to a solution. Once a needs assessment establishes that there is problem to resolve or a policy goal worth pursuing, different solutions can be considered. This is where theory connects various types of projects or activities to strategic goals.
- Level 2, "design and theory," focuses specifically on the design of a policy, project, or activity.
- Level 3, "process and implementation," concerns the execution of the elements prescribed by the design and theory in level 2.
- Level 4, "outcome and impact," measures the changes (often long-term) that ultimately result from the program's efforts.
- Level 5, "cost-effectiveness," assesses the relative value gained from the program as compared with other, similar efforts.

We think of these five aspects, integral to the assessment framework, as a hierarchy, depicted graphically in Figure 1.1.

In this hierarchy, a positive assessment at a higher level relies on positive assessments at the lower levels. By "positive," we mean that the assessment reveals that associated objectives are being met. Accordingly, problems at a higher level of the hierarchy link to problems at lower levels of the hierarchy. For example, if a cost-effectiveness assessment reveals a problem, examining information from the lower levels of the hierarchy will lead to the root cause of the problem.

In the fourth task of the study, the RAND team collated the findings from the survey analysis and provided those findings and other observations to the sponsor. Based on the survey findings, we developed specific recommendations and identified key elements of an assessment implementation plan for the sponsor's consideration, the fifth task of the study.

Figure 1.1
Five Levels: The Assessment Hierarchy

SOURCE: Adapted from Rossi, Lipsey, and Freeman, 2004, Exhibit 3-C. Used with permission.
NOTE: For a detailed discussion of the assessment hierarchy, see Paul et al., 2006.
RAND TR1121-1.1

Particular attention was paid to any identified gaps that might limit the ability of OUSD(P) to assess the 1206 Program.

This report lays the groundwork for a comprehensive assessment of the 1206 Program rather than for various "snapshot-in-time" assessments of specific 1206 projects around the world. It takes a longer-term view, with the understanding that accurate assessments, especially those focused on outcomes and cost-effectiveness, require time and effort. However, without well-informed knowledge of what does and does not work in terms of security cooperation, program managers and policymakers will be unable to make educated decisions regarding 1206 Program expenditures.

Organization of This Report

Chapter Two provides an overview of the RAND team's security cooperation and assessment construct and explains why assessment is important, how to think about assessments, how security cooperation assessments should be conducted, and the utility of assessment results in informing decisionmaking. Chapter Three discusses the results of focused interviews that the team conducted with key 1206 Program stakeholders in OUSD(P), DSCA, DoS, the COCOMs, the military services, and Congress, identifying five key insights that helped shape the recommendations presented later in this report. Chapter Four examines the results of the 1206 Program survey analysis conducted by the RAND team. Chapter Five presents five key findings and nine key recommendations resulting from the analysis, as well as details on the key components of an assessment implementation plan along two parallel tracks.

It is important to note that this study draws on previous RAND research sponsored by the Office of the Deputy Assistant Secretary of Defense for Partnership Strategy and Stability Operations, the U.S. Air Force, and the U.S. Army and documented in the following publications:

- *Developing an Assessment Framework for U.S. Air Force Building Partnerships Programs*, by Jennifer D. P. Moroney, Joe Hogler, Jefferson P. Marquis, Christopher Paul, John E. Peters, and Beth Grill, Santa Monica, Calif.: RAND Corporation, MG-868-AF, 2010.
- *Adding Value to Air Force Management Through Building Partnerships Assessment*, by Jefferson P. Marquis, Joe Hogler, Jennifer D. P. Moroney, Michael J. Neumann, Christopher Paul, John E. Peters, Gregory F. Treverton, and Anny Wong, Santa Monica, Calif.: RAND Corporation, TR-907-AF, 2010.
- *Developing an Army Strategy for Building Partner Capacity for Stability Operations*, Jefferson P. Marquis, Jennifer D. P. Moroney, Justin Beck, Derek Eaton, Scott Hiromoto, David R. Howell, Janet Lewis, Charlotte Lynch, Michael J. Neumann, and Cathryn Quantic Thurston, Santa Monica, Calif.: RAND Corporation, MG-942-A, 2010.
- *A Framework to Assess Programs for Building Partnerships*, by Jennifer D. P. Moroney, Jefferson P. Marquis, Cathryn Quantic Thurston, and Gregory F. Treverton, Santa Monica, Calif.: RAND Corporation, MG-863-OSD, 2009.
- *Building Partner Capacity to Combat Weapons of Mass Destruction*, by Jennifer D. P. Moroney and Joe Hogler, with Benjamin Bahney, Kim Cragin, David R. Howell, Charlotte Lynch, and S. Rebecca Zimmerman, Santa Monica, Calif.: RAND Corporation, MG-783-DTRA, 2009.

CHAPTER TWO

RAND's Assessment Framework

This chapter provides an overview of the RAND team's security cooperation and building partnerships assessment construct and argues for the relevance and importance of assessment for the 1206 Program. This chapter draws heavily on recently published RAND research for the U.S. Air Force and OUSD(P) on security cooperation assessment frameworks, as mentioned in Chapter One, which explain why assessment is important, how to think about assessments, how security cooperation assessments should be conducted, and the utility of assessment results in informing decisionmaking. The chapter begins by explaining the basic rationale for conducting security cooperation assessments and provides some examples of ongoing challenges to assessment in this area. It then explains how the framework connects to the key insights presented later in this report.

What Is Assessment?

Assessment is research or analysis to inform decisionmaking. When most people think of evaluation or assessment, they tend to think of outcomes assessment: Does the object of the assessment "work"? Is it worthwhile? While this is certainly within the purview of assessment, assessments cover a much broader range.

Most assessments require using research methods common in the social sciences. However, assessment is distinguished from other forms of research in terms of purpose. Assessment is fundamentally action-oriented. Assessments are conducted to determine the value, worth, or impact of a policy, program, proposal, practice, design, or service with a view toward making change decisions about that program or program element in the future. In short, *assessments must explicitly connect to informing decisionmaking.*

Within the action-oriented or decision-support role, assessments can vary widely. They can support decisions to adjust, expand, contract, or terminate a program, project, or activity. They can support decisions regarding which services a project should deliver and to whom. Assessments can also support decisions about how to manage and execute a program or program elements.

Why Assess?

Although some decisions are based on ad hoc or intuitive assessments, others demand assessments that incorporate more extensive or rigorous research methods, particularly when the program involves large resource commitments. Where there are important decisions to be made and ambiguities exist about the factual bases for those decisions, assessment is the antidote.

Across most aspects of government and military activity, there are regular calls for assessments; the 1206 Program is no exception. For example, DoD and DoS are required to submit an annual report to Congress that assesses the status of projects under way or completed during the prior year. COCOMs and component commands also conduct assessments of COCOM theater campaign plans (TCPs) throughout the year. Although these assessments are typically carried out at the TCP objective or country level, 1206 Program resources are an important contributor to many of these assessments.

Additionally, in 2010, a new office was established in the Office of the Deputy Assistant Secretary of Defense for Partnership Strategy and Stability Operations within OUSD(P) to develop an approach to assessing the security cooperation programs that OUSD(P) directly manages, including the 1206 Program and several others, such as the DoD Regional Centers, the Counterterrorism Fellowship Program, and the Warsaw Initiative Fund.[1] Answering questions as to the real or anticipated outcome of DoD security cooperation programs has become commonplace throughout the DoD policymaking community.

Challenges to 1206 Program Assessment

We would be remiss not to discuss the challenges to conducting assessments with regard to security cooperation more broadly and the 1206 Program in particular. These challenges are not insurmountable; some are endemic and some are more focused on process. However, it is important to keep them in mind to find solutions or develop workarounds that will enable DoD to implement desired assessment processes.

Determining Causality
Arguably, the biggest challenge confronting assessment in this area lies in trying to identify causality: linking specific 1206 projects and activities to specific progress toward program goals, broader COCOM or U.S. objectives, and end states (outcomes).[2] The abundance of initiatives in the broader realm of U.S. security cooperation—in DoS, other DoD programs, the U.S. Agency for International Development, and the Departments of Justice, Homeland Security, Energy, Treasury, and Commerce—confound our ability to assign causality, as do various exogenous factors, such as international politics, global public diplomacy, and partner nations themselves. The best we can hope for at the outcomes level, in many instances, is to find some relationship between success in the 1206 Program and progress in security cooperation focus areas.

Well-Articulated Intermediate Goals to Inform Decisionmaking
As stated previously, assessments are tied to decisionmaking. However, a critical assessment challenge is identifying the information on which decisions should be based. For example, it is fairly intuitive to decide whether or not to continue a project or activity based on whether

---

[1]   See key recommendations made in Moroney, Marquis, et al., 2009.

[2]   See Marquis, Moroney, et al., 2010, Appendix D.

or not it is achieving its objectives. However, it is analytically very difficult to tell whether something is working when causal connections are conflated with other activities or end states and when goals are very high-level, opaque, or difficult to measure or when they require that a program or activity contribute only indirectly. Well-articulated intermediate goals to which programs can directly contribute are important for effective program assessment. However, where such goals are lacking, decisions are difficult to support with assessment.

This connects directly to one of the five key organizational insights presented in this report: the need to establish measurable objectives that explicitly connect to broader U.S. government, theater, regional, and 1206 Program goals.

Assessment Capabilities of 1206 Program Stakeholders

Effort is required for both the collection of raw data and the analysis needed to produce completed assessments. Resource constraints can adversely affect the quality of data collection. Different organizations have differing levels of preparation and capability for assessment. Some 1206 Program stakeholders have access to personnel who can help with assessment or have sufficient staffing (and foresight) to provide dedicated assessment personnel. Other stakeholder offices are very tightly staffed, with just a few personnel already wearing multiple hats and working long hours before assessment even enters the picture.

The 1206 Program is a mixed bag in this regard. Good assessment planning and assessment matching can ease the resource burden. Relevant personnel will be better able to plan for and complete assessment data collection if they know about it before the period or event for which they will collect data. A single set of coherent assessment data requests requires less time to complete than a host of different and partially duplicative or partially useless assessment data calls.

While Chapter Four provides greater detail about current capabilities to collect data and conduct assessment among 1206 Program stakeholders, three needed improvements in this area connect directly to several of the key insights and will help address this challenge: the need to provide formal guidance on assessment processes, the need to establish 1206 Program assessment roles and responsibilities, and the need to set data collection and reporting requirements.

Multiplicity of and Differing Priorities of Stakeholders

The 1206 Program has a host of different stakeholders. Decisions for and about the program and its projects and activities are made by many different organizations and at many different levels. The constellation of stakeholders varies by region and organizational level. Although the inclusion of many stakeholders is not inherently challenging, it can complicate assessments in a number of ways. For example, personnel at the project execution level can have multiple masters with different goals. 1206 Program projects are typically designed by COCOM planners to help support the achievement of TCP objectives, but they are often executed by military service organizations that are focused on compliance with acquisition regulations and technology transfer legislation. These competing goals can complicate assessment when different stakeholders request different but similar assessments using different processes.

Security Cooperation Data Tracking Systems Are Not Currently Organized for 1206 Program Assessment

DoD and U.S. government security cooperation programs and funding are widely dispersed in terms of who is responsible for them. Some security cooperation data are maintained in the

COCOMs' respective Theater Security Cooperation Management Information Systems, but not all 1206 Program stakeholders provide input, nor do they all have access to these systems. As a result, it is not clear that a complete, accurate, or current repository of 1206 Program projects and activities and their details (e.g., resources involved, place, duration, frequency) exists. COCOMs have created new databases to track 1206 Program inputs, but generally, these databases are used only for internal purposes and are not tied to assessing the overall effect of the program in specific countries.

Delegating Assessment Responsibilities

There is also the practice, widespread in DoD, of delegating the task of assessment to subordinate organizations. Although this practice may be effective at the upper echelons of OUSD(P), it can cause trouble for multiple reasons. The first problem is that many of the officers and staffers charged with this responsibility lack the skills to design and perform assessments. Often, without an assessment template and a dataset at hand, they must conceive and execute the assessment without any high-level guidance. Even in organizations with appropriately trained staff, the necessary data are rarely fully available, and potential sources are not obvious.

Unless 1206 Program guidance documents specify the types of assessments expected from particular commands, agencies, offices, or organizations and outlines steps to collect and organize the supporting information, individual offices will have little choice but to continue the common practice of polling subject-matter experts for their opinions of how various projects and activities have performed. The instinct behind approaching subject-matter or functional experts is correct, but without proper assessment guidance, the effort will be ad hoc at best.

Expectations and Preconceived Notions of Assessment

A final challenge inherent in 1206 Program assessment stems from the expectations and preconceived notions of many stakeholders. There are many different views about what assessment is or should be. Virtually all military officers and senior civilians have some experience with assessment, but usually just a limited slice of what is possible under the broad tent offered by evaluation research. A narrow preconception that assessment is only ever one type of analysis or data collection can be limiting. Further, expectations that assessment adds limited value or that it is acceptable to require assessments to satisfy curiosity (rather than inform essential decisions) can lead to unnecessary evaluations or create resistance to assessment proposals.

In fact, assessment is many different things from many different perspectives. Virtually all of these perspectives—provided they pertain to decisionmaking—are captured in the hierarchy of evaluation, described next.

Levels of Assessment: The Hierarchy of Evaluation

Given the explicit focus on assessment for decisionmaking that comes from evaluation research and the necessity of connecting stakeholders and their decisionmaking needs with specific types of assessment, OUSD(P) needs a unifying framework to facilitate that matching process. To fill this need, we present "the hierarchy of evaluation" as developed by evaluation researchers

Peter Rossi, Mark Lipsey, and Howard Freeman (see Figure 1.1 in Chapter One).[3] The RAND team found this to be the most useful model of those available in the literature. The hierarchy divides all potential evaluations and assessments into five nested levels. Each higher level is predicated on success at a lower level. For example, positive assessments of cost-effectiveness (the highest level) are only possible if supported by positive assessments at all other levels. We elaborate on this concept in the section "Hierarchy and Nesting," later in this chapter.

Level 1: Assessment of Need for the Program

Level 1, at the bottom of the hierarchy and serving as its foundation, is the assessment of the need for the program or activity. This is where evaluation connects most explicitly with target ends or goals. Evaluation at this level focuses on solving the problem and determining the goal(s) to be met, the population to be served, and the kinds of services that might contribute to a solution.[4] In the context of the 1206 Program, this level of assessment is perhaps best applied at the project proposal stage. During the proposal review process, Office of the Secretary of Defense (OSD), Joint Staff, and DoS program managers use the following assessment questions:

- What is the terrorist threat?
- What is the capability gap?
- What is the consequence of not conducting the assessment?
- Do the training and equipment requested fill the capability gap?

For DoD, the need for the overall 1206 Program is not what is being explored; instead, program managers and other stakeholders might consider assessing the need for individual projects or collections of interrelated projects. For example, consider a project that proposes to provide a partner with a maritime counterterrorism capability. Additional potential assessment questions include the following:

- What is the nature and magnitude of the terrorist threat?
- What audience, population, or targets does the need apply to (e.g., maritime border patrol, Navy)?
- What kinds of services or activities are needed to address the problem?
- What existing programs or activities contribute to meeting this goal or mitigating this problem?
- What are the goals and objectives to be met through the project?
- What are the risks of not taking action?

Evaluation of public policy often skips the needs-assessment level, as stakeholders assume the need to be wholly obvious. This is true broadly in public policy, but also in DoD. Where such a need is genuinely obvious or the policy assumptions are strong, this is not problematic. Where need is not obvious or goals are not well articulated, troubles starting at level 1 in the evaluation hierarchy can complicate assessment at each higher level.

---

[3] Rossi, Lipsey, and Freeman, 2004.

[4] Rossi, Lipsey, and Freeman, 2004, p. 76.

Level 2: Assessment of Design and Theory

The assessment of concept, design, and theory is the second level in the hierarchy. Once a needs assessment establishes that there is problem or policy goal to pursue, as well as the intended objectives of such policy, different solutions can be considered. *This is where theory connects ways to ends.* In developing a project proposal to address the maritime security example, one might consider the various types of activities that might be undertaken to achieve the objective of providing a counterterrorism capability from a design and theory perspective. Equipment such as small craft, uniforms, small arms, or radios might be desired, as would the training necessary for their operation. Exercises conducted with U.S. forces to demonstrate the capability might be a culminating activity, and the establishment of an ongoing bilateral working group to discuss further progress might also be appropriate. While all of these activities may sound logical, a deeper assessment of the design and the theory behind them is essential.

Assessment at this level focuses on the design of the project and its activities and should begin immediately as a way to ensure that the project is sound from the beginning. Analyses of alternatives are generally evaluations at this level and can be useful in determining the best approach. Research questions might include the following:

- What types of activities are appropriate for providing and sustaining a counterterrorism capability?
- What specific services are needed, in what quantity, and for how long?
- How can these services best be delivered?
- What outputs (e.g., training, equipment deliveries) need to be produced?
- How should the project and its activities be organized and managed?
- What resources will be required for the project and its activities?
- Is the theory specifying certain services as solutions to the target problem sound?
- What is the partner's ability to absorb the assistance?
- Will the partner be willing to employ the capability?

The hierarchy bases most of the evaluation questions at this level on theory or on previous experience with similar efforts. This is a critical level in the hierarchy. If project design is based on poor theory, then perfect execution (the ways) may still not bring about the desired results (the ends). Similarly, if the theory does not actually connect the ways with the ends, the program may accomplish objectives other than the stated ones. Unfortunately, assessors often omit this step or restrict their efforts at this level of evaluation by making unfounded assumptions, an issue addressed in more detail later.

Once an effort is under way, design and theory can be assessed firsthand. For example, once the maritime equipment has been delivered and training has commenced, assessment questions at this level could include the following:

- Are the services provided adequate in duration and quantity?
- Is the frequency with which the services are provided adequate?
- Are resources sufficient for the desired execution?

Note that assessments at this level are not about execution (i.e., "Are the services being provided as designed?"). Such questions are asked at the next level, level 3. Design and theory assessments (level 2) seek to confirm that what was *planned* is adequate to achieve the desired objectives. In other words, the question is not whether the boats have been delivered but rather, "Were boats the right solution to the problem?"

Level 3: Assessment of Process and Implementation

Level 3 in the hierarchy of evaluation focuses on program operations and the execution of the elements prescribed by the theory and design in level 2. A program can be perfectly executed but still not achieve its goals if the design was inadequate. Conversely, poor execution can foil the most brilliant design. In the case of the maritime security example, a well-designed activity to provide small maritime patrol craft could fail to achieve the desired results if not supported by adequate training or plans for sustainment and maintenance.

Assessment at this level needs to be periodic and ongoing. In addition to measuring the effectiveness of processes, level 3 evaluations also include an assessment of outputs, i.e., the quantifiable deliverables of an effort. Such evaluations might include an assessment of the timeliness of the Foreign Military Sales (FMS) program's process, as well as the accuracy of the equipment delivered. Possible research questions at this level include the following:

- Were the necessary resources made available?
- Are the intended services, such as training and equipment, being delivered as designed?
- Are process and administrative objectives, such as those of the FMS process, being met?
- Is the activity being managed well?
- Is the partner nation satisfied with the equipment and training?
- Were applicable security assistance manuals and regulations followed?
- Are resources being used or consumed as intended?

Level 4: Assessment of Outcome and Impact

Level 4 is near the top of the evaluation hierarchy and concerns outcomes and impact. At this level, the hierarchy translates outputs into outcomes, a level of performance, or achievement. This translation must contain enough detail to explain the path from specific activities to specific capabilities. Put another way, *outputs* are the products of program activities, and *outcomes* are the changes resulting from the projects. In practical terms, one might be interested in assessing whether or not the partner nation has actually achieved a counterterrorism capability. Determining how well the combination of equipment, training, exercises, and sustainment provisions has translated to a real capability is the essence of this type of assessment. This is the first level of assessment that examines how well the solutions have addressed the problem that originally motivated the effort. Research questions at level 4 in this example could include the following:

- Do the patrol craft and trained crews provide benefits to the recipients in terms of countering terrorism?
- Did the training result in proficient crews that are able to engage in counterterrorism operations?
- Are program objectives and goals being achieved?
- Is the terrorism problem at which the project or activity is targeted being addressed sufficiently?

Level 5: Assessment of Cost-Effectiveness

The assessment of cost-effectiveness sits at the top of the evaluation hierarchy, at level 5. Efforts to assess cost-effectiveness are possible when at least partially observable desired outcomes are present.

Evaluations at this level are often most attractive in bottom-line terms but depend heavily on data collected over time at the lower levels of evaluation. It can be complicated to measure cost-effectiveness in situations in which unclear resource flows or exogenous factors significantly affect outcomes. As the highest level of evaluation, this assessment depends on the lower levels and can provide feedback inputs for policy decisions primarily based on the lower levels. For example, if target levels of cost-efficiency are not met, cost data (level 5) in conjunction with process data (level 3) can be used to streamline the process or otherwise selectively reduce costs. Put another way, if the training on small craft procedures is too costly, then perhaps the training process is not efficient, or perhaps the partner simply cannot absorb the training (a level 2 issue regarding the design and theory of the program). Alternatively, the design (level 2) could be the problem. To repeat an earlier but important point, the levels of assessment are nested, and resolving issues such as cost-effectiveness relies heavily on understanding how the program is functioning at other levels. Possible level 5 research questions include the following:

- How efficient is resource expenditure versus outcome realized?
- Is the cost reasonable relative to the magnitude of benefits?
- Could alternative approaches yield comparable benefits at a lower cost?

Hierarchy and Nesting

This framework is a hierarchy because the levels nest with each other; solutions to problems observed at higher levels of assessment often lie at levels below. If the desired outcomes (level 4) are achieved at the desired levels of cost-effectiveness (level 5), then lower levels of evaluation are irrelevant. But what about when they are not?

When desired high-level outcomes are *not* achieved, information from the lower levels of assessment needs to be available to be examined. For example, if an effort is not realizing target outcomes, is that because the process is not being executed as designed (level 3) or because the effort was not designed well (level 2)? Evaluators have problems when an assessment scheme does not include evaluations at a sufficiently low level to inform effective policy decisions and diagnose problems when the program does not perform as intended. Assuming away the lowest levels of evaluation is only acceptable if the assumptions prove correct. However, when assumptions are questionable, the best risk-avoidance strategy is to conduct assessments at levels 1 and 2 rather than launching a program that will fail at levels 4 and 5 because the critical levels simply will not support overall targets. According to Rossi, Lipsey, and Freeman, programs that fail generally do so because of problems at level 2 (theory) or level 3 (implementation).[5] Good program implementation works only if the underlying program design works.

---

[5] Rossi, Lipsey, and Freeman, 2004, p. 78.

Key Insights and the Assessment Framework

As previously noted, this report refers to five key insights that the study team drew from the results of this research effort. These insights were used to guide the development of the assessment implementation plan in Chapter Five. They are as follows:

1. Provide formal guidance on the assessment process.
2. Set measurable objectives that explicitly connect to broader U.S. government, theater, regional, and 1206 Program goals.
3. Establish 1206 Program assessment roles and responsibilities.
4. Set data collection and reporting requirements.
5. Improve coordination with key agencies.

In the following section, we discuss only three of them (numbers 2, 3, and 4) as they relate explicitly and directly to the RAND team's assessment. Providing guidance and improving coordination are important aspects of implementing an assessment framework more broadly but do not relate directly to the assessment hierarchy.

Assessment and Objectives

As noted earlier, clear objectives are critical for successful assessment. Decisionmaking above the program management level relies on assessments at level 4 (outcome and impact) and level 5 (cost-effectiveness). It is virtually impossible to assess the success of an undertaking (outcome) unless the intended objective of that effort is clear. Objectives should be clear at each level of activity and should nest and clearly connect. In the 1206 Program context, this means that broad program goals should be clearly articulated and communicated to stakeholders, and ideally should connect explicitly to broader security cooperation goals provided by the National Security Strategy, the National Defense Strategy, the National Military Strategy, the Guidance for the Employment of the Force (GEF), and COCOM TCPs and functional campaign plans. Specific projects and activities should, in turn, have clearly stated objectives that connect explicitly to program-level objectives.

Clear objectives make higher-level (levels 4 and 5) assessments possible, but they also facilitate lower-level assessments. For example, if objectives are clear and nest from lower to higher levels, design and theory are more likely to be explicit in the connections, enabling more transparency at that level (level 2). In this way, effective assessment guidance connects to and hinges on broader program guidance regarding program objectives and the establishment of objectives for program projects and activities.

Assessment Roles and Responsibilities

In general, there are four functional assessment roles that need to be performed with respect to 1206 Program assessment. The following are definitions for the four stakeholder assessment functions identified in prior RAND research:[6]

---

6   See Moroney, Hogler, et al., 2010.

- *Data collector.* Responsible for collecting and aggregating data for a particular kind of assessment from internal and external sources according to standards set by the assessor organization.
- *Assessor.* Responsible for setting data collection standards for a particular kind of assessment and for conducting evaluations using methods suitable for the types of assessment being performed.
- *Reviewer.* Responsible for helping assessors to develop data collection standards and evaluation methods that are appropriate for the type of assessment being performed, as well as for conducting periodic inspections or audits to ensure that assessments are being properly executed.
- *Integrator.* Responsible for organizing and synthesizing programmatic assessments to meet assessment requirements and feed into decisionmaking processes.

We intend for these roles to help guide assessment behavior, not to restrict the range of assignments that a particular organization or office is allowed to undertake. In many cases, assigning specific responsibilities to particular organizations will require looking beyond traditional practices. In particular, it is important to pay close attention to an organization's *capabilities*, especially its resources, expertise (in terms of both subject matter and function, e.g., acquisition, accounting, legal), proximity, and opportunity. It is also critically important to note its *objectivity*, i.e., the extent of its interest in specific assessment results. This consideration will facilitate a move away from the current, largely ad hoc self-assessment approach.

There are some key principles in assigning stakeholder assessment roles:

- Delineate assessment responsibilities across several stakeholders to account for different levels of organizational authority and expertise and to inject as much objectivity into the process as possible.
- Identify a single organization with a close connection to the activity at hand to be ultimately responsible for gathering and collating assessment data. Note, however, that data collection will often involve a number of individuals and organizations from different parts of DoD (and even from outside).
- Recognize that, in some cases, the data collector and the assessor will be the same individual; more likely, these positions will be held by persons in the same organization.
- Ensure that the assessor and the reviewer are not the same person; they may be within the same organization, but this is not ideal.
- Ensure that reviewers (especially) and integrators pay careful attention to which data are collected and which attributes are selected as outputs and outcomes, lest attributes be designed to fit what the program has done and not necessarily its goals.
- Maintain strong linkages between integrators and program stakeholders to develop as much standardization as possible and to foster clarity on best practices in security cooperation assessment.
- Integrators should develop mechanisms for storing assessment information (so that it is available to as wide a group of program stakeholders as possible) and synthesizing this information for various decisionmaking purposes.

Data Collection and Reporting

It is not enough to specify who has a data collection role. It is important to clarify what data are needed, how to collect and format the data, where they should be sent, and when they are due. To function optimally, such collection must be structured, and it must be mandatory. When data are late or absent, or collected or reported in an inconsistent manner, it can make the assessor's job more difficult (if not impossible).

Conclusion

Assessment is a challenging but critical tool to effectively support decisionmaking within and about the 1206 Program. The framework presented here intends to aid in the assessment process by breaking down a complex task into its various components. The discussion of the framework illustrates how to take a theoretical structure and tailor it to a specific program by linking it with concrete program objectives. Specifically, 1206 Program assessment processes need to include measurable objectives, the clear assignment of assessment roles and responsibilities, and collection and reporting requirements for data collection in support of all five levels of the hierarchy of evaluation.

Exploring the Options for 1206 Program Assessment: Discussions with Key Stakeholders

Most policymakers, military and defense planners, and project implementers perceive the 1206 Global Train and Equip Program as a unique security cooperation program. Its focus on urgent and emergent threats and building partner-nation capabilities for counterterrorism and stability operations has created new opportunities for partner engagement and led to closer interagency cooperation. In the four years since the inception of the 1206 Program, primary stakeholders have adopted new roles and responsibilities for implementing the program. Moreover, although they have also begun to develop methods of internal data collection and assessment, they have not participated in a comprehensive, program-wide assessment.

To understand better how the 1206 Program is currently implemented and to identify stakeholders and sources of data that could be used to support future assessments, the RAND study team interviewed stakeholders drawn from a broad range of U.S. government participants at various levels. The information gained from these interviews was then used to develop the structured assessment survey discussed in Chapter Four.

This chapter describes how the team conducted the interviews and provides a summary of stakeholder perceptions of the strengths and weaknesses of the 1206 Program and its current implementation process. It then presents stakeholder observations as they relate to the insights derived from the assessment framework.

Stakeholder Interviews

Members of the RAND study team conducted a series of 14 semistructured interviews with key stakeholders in the U.S. government to ascertain current roles in the 1206 Program, as well as to identify data sources and existing assessment processes for the program. The research team conducted in-person and telephone discussions with key individuals engaged in the planning, administration, and oversight of the 1206 Program. Interviewees included representatives from five geographic COCOMs,[1] U.S. Special Operations Command, OUSD(P), DSCA, the U.S. Joint Chiefs of Staff Office of Strategic Plans and Policy (J5), U.S. Army Security Assistance Command, the Navy International Programs Office, the Office of the Deputy Under Secretary of the Air Force for International Affairs, the Bureau of Political-Military Affairs in DoS, and four congressional committees. A total of 30 individuals participated in 14 separate

---

[1] U.S. Africa Command (USAFRICOM), U.S. Central Command (USCENTCOM), U.S. European Command (USEUCOM), U.S. Pacific Command (USPACOM), and U.S. Southern Command (USSOUTHCOM).

interviews (see Appendix B). We do not attribute interview responses to specific offices or individuals in this chapter.

During the interviews, we asked stakeholders to describe their roles, responsibilities, and experience with the 1206 Program. We asked both planners and implementers about the objectives of the 1206 Program projects with which they were involved and how they determined whether they were achieving these objectives. We also inquired about the aspects of 1206 Program projects that they found to be most successful based on their personal experience, as well as those aspects that posed the greatest challenges. In addition, we requested that stakeholders offer their suggestions for developing and implementing a new assessment process. The results of these interviews were used to inform both the structured online survey that is described in Chapter Four (and presented in Appendix A) and the overall conclusions and recommendations presented in Chapter Five.

Stakeholder Perceptions of the 1206 Program

During our interviews, 1206 Program stakeholders identified a number of important issue areas, discussed in this section. Stakeholders from OUSD(P), DSCA, DoS, the COCOMs, and the services expressed a common understanding of the goals and objectives of the 1206 Program. They emphasized the program's focus on "urgent and emergent" threats as well as building partner-nation capacity for counterterrorism and stability operations. Most noted that the program is supposed to reflect COCOM needs while maintaining a narrow focus on activities that directly support current U.S. security objectives. Moreover, nearly all stakeholders commented that the program required increased cooperation between agencies (particularly between DoS and DoD).

They noted, however, that there are both strengths and weaknesses in the current implementation of the 1206 Program, particularly regarding the one-year timeline, program sustainability, the process of project design and selection, and interagency cooperation. Many stakeholders also commented that although they believed that the implementation process had improved over time, there was no formal assessment procedure in place to evaluate either the implementation process or program outcomes. Although some offices or commands have conducted internal assessments, they are typically informal, not comprehensive, and not shared with other stakeholders. Stakeholders provided a number of suggestions for developing an effective, comprehensive assessment framework, described at the end of this chapter, that could build on existing mechanisms for data collection.

Short Timeline Allows Faster Impact but Creates Administrative Difficulties
Stakeholders stated that the short timeline dictated by the 1206 Program's legal authority creates both positive and negative effects. The requirement that 1206 Program funding be obligated by the end of the fiscal year forces offices to prioritize tasks related to 1206 Program execution, enabling 1206 Program projects to be implemented relatively quickly. They noted that this accelerated implementation has, in turn, allowed the 1206 Program to have a more immediate effect on partner-nation capabilities than other initiatives funded by FMS or other security assistance programs. COCOM stakeholders noted that while other security assistance projects often take three to four years to process, under the 1206 Program, partner nations have received equipment such as night-vision goggles and communication hardware in less

than a year. COCOM stakeholders also noted that the focus on "urgent and emergent" threats as a guideline for 1206 Program funding facilitates partnership capacity-building projects that would not otherwise be possible under other authorities, in terms of both the type of equipment and training provided and the selection of recipient countries. For example, countries that otherwise would not have received priority for security cooperation funds, such as those facing emerging threats in Africa, have received much-needed training and equipment through 1206 funds. Additionally, the 1206 Program facilitated the provision of equipment for counterterrorism missions and training for stability operations in Afghanistan that might not otherwise have been available to partner nations.

At the same time, most stakeholders observed that the abbreviated timelines of the 1206 Program could create significant administrative difficulties. Short deadlines often leave less time for planning and can lead to "sloppiness" in the preparation of project proposals, according to those who review and implement the proposals. The process for executing 1206 Program projects follows that of the pseudo–case system used in the FMS program, which is not designed to function within the single fiscal-year time frame required by the 1206 Program authority. The complexities of the approval and acquisition process require DSCA and the services to request special legal exemptions to the standard contracting process for many of the programs selected for funding. Additionally, the services may face difficulties in facilitating equipment orders within the fiscal year time frame, particularly when aircraft or military vehicles are involved. These items require significant groundwork in developing and validating cases and completing the contracts required to transfer them to partner nations.

The short time frame also makes staffing to support the 1206 Program a challenge. Stakeholders at all levels noted the difficulty in accommodating the increased workload necessary to administer the program without additional staff, and 1206 Program roles are therefore treated as an additional temporary duty by most offices. Long-term civilian employees able to observe 1206 Program projects over time may alleviate this problem and provide continuity. Some service representatives questioned whether the workload was out of proportion compared with the dollar value of the program appropriation.

Lack of Funding for Maintenance and Support Creates Concerns About Sustainability

The sustainability of 1206 Program funding was a concern raised by many stakeholders during our interviews. One COCOM representative indicated that, because the focus on counterterrorism is particularly relevant to both the United States and many partner nations, participating partner nations have a greater interest in maintaining new capabilities acquired through the 1206 Program, as compared with other types of capabilities or materiel.[2] However, stakeholders also noted that the absence of a requirement for partner nations to contribute their own resources for the training and equipment is a potential impediment to the sustainability of the 1206 Program, as some partner nations lack both the commitment and the resources required to support new capabilities over time.

Several stakeholders also expressed concern that once partner nations receive 1206 Program funding, they may develop an appetite for training and equipment that is not sustain-

---

[2]   When the 1206 Program commenced in 2006, there was no provision for additional funding for maintenance and training beyond the initial award. Although the use of follow-on funding for maintenance was approved beginning in 2007, many stakeholders nonetheless expressed concern about a potential lack of dedicated funding for maintenance and support by the 1206 authority, which, in turn, would limit the long-term sustainability of efforts to build partner-nation capacity.

able through other funding mechanisms, leaving partner nations frustrated when faced with uncertainty about funding from year to year. For some partner nations, 1206 Program funds represent a small percentage of overall U.S. security assistance, but for others, particularly African nations, 1206 Program funds are a primary source of security assistance. Other stakeholders noted that the 1206 Program's expedited delivery schedules have given partner nations unrealistic expectations for rapid implementation of other U.S. security assistance programs, including FMS.

The Project Design, Selection, Prioritization, and Assessment Processes Are Somewhat Unclear

When asked about the process for designing and selecting individual projects, a number of stakeholders indicated that U.S. security objectives are a primary consideration. Noting this as a strength, they commented that the United States has greater influence over the type of equipment and training provided through the 1206 Program as compared with other programs that accommodate partner-nation interests, such as FMS. This, in turn, allows the United States to build capabilities through the 1206 Program that support U.S. national security objectives.[3]

Despite general agreement among stakeholders that 1206 Program spending directly supports U.S. national security objectives, some of those interviewed expressed confusion over the specific definition of those objectives and how, in turn, individual 1206 Program projects are selected. Some stakeholders indicated that they did not know which policy and planning office defines priorities for 1206 Program funding, nor had they seen a written articulation of those priorities. Some OUSD(P), DSCA, and COCOM stakeholders also noted that the process of project selection has changed over time, with fewer projects proposals originating from the COCOMs; however, those that are submitted are more in line with OUSD(P) guidance.[4] A small number of the stakeholders we interviewed remarked that policy planners in the Pentagon steered the 1206 Program project funding toward countries that are a high priority for policymakers.[5]

Interagency Cooperation Has Improved, but Data Sharing Is Limited

Nearly all stakeholders believed that communication and collaboration between DoD and DoS had improved as a result of the 1206 Program. Many noted that the "dual-key" nature of the 1206 Program authority requires greater interagency cooperation at various levels, and several remarked that this was, in fact, the most successful aspect of the program. Some stakeholders commented that since the initiation of the 1206 Program, they are "always on the phone" with their counterparts in other agencies and now meet regularly through interagency working groups.

One model of improved coordination noted by a COCOM representative was the creation of a "contract integrator" position in the field. This contracted position is dedicated to supporting security cooperation officers in overseeing the training and equipping of programs

---

[3] One stakeholder explained that high-end capabilities, such as the F-16, are often on the top of partner-nation "shopping lists" but are not as useful as helicopters for building counterterrorism capabilities.

[4] After OUSD(P) issues its annual guidance for project proposals, COCOMs submit proposals for 1206 Program funds. These proposals are reviewed and prioritized in separate but parallel processes by a working group of program administrators in OASD(SO/LIC&IC) and the Bureau of Political-Military Affairs in DoS.

[5] Lebanon and Yemen were two examples cited in multiple interviews.

in various partner nations. The contract integrator helps ensure communication between the facilitators of different 1206 Program projects and between the COCOM, the services, and DoS.

Still, many stakeholders expressed a need for better coordination in the contracting process and greater transparency in program reporting. For example, COCOMs are rarely notified when the equipment they have requested has been shipped, which has occasionally resulted in the mistaken return of unclaimed items. For its part, OUSD(P) is rarely notified whether equipment or training has been delivered, let alone informed as to whether a given project has met its stated objectives. Several stakeholders noted the need for better coordination as an issue that negatively affects current efforts to conduct assessments. When asked whether their individual offices conducted any form of internal assessment, several OUSD(P), DSCA, COCOM, and service representatives indicated that they had created informal systems to track outputs or process milestones within their areas of responsibility (AORs). These "assessments" (or data collection initiatives, as we would classify them) tended to focus on monitoring internal departmental procedures rather than evaluating project outcomes.

Some stakeholders noted that recent efforts have been made to improve data sharing through conferences, workshops, and data portals; however, there was no formal mechanism for coordinating these ad hoc processes. Current data collection requirements—to the extent that they exist—do not require 1206 Program stakeholders to share any of the data that they collect with other stakeholders, contributing to a lack of transparency among participating offices.

Stakeholder Observations Relative to Insights of Assessment

Although most stakeholders shared a general perception that execution of the 1206 Program has improved over time, there was also broad recognition of the need for a more formal assessment process both to substantiate the continued need for the program and to identify ways to improve its execution. The study team asked stakeholders to share their thoughts on what information a future program-wide assessment might capture and which stakeholders would be best suited to provide the necessary data. Although interviewers did not introduce the framework described in Chapter Two, we have structured the subjects' responses to illustrate the insights derived from the assessment framework.

Guidance on Assessment Is Needed

Stakeholders agreed on the urgent need for a comprehensive, multilayered assessment of the 1206 Program. Most of those interviewed were aware of (and many had contributed to) reviews of the 1206 Program conducted by congressional delegations or external research agencies, such as GAO, the Congressional Research Service, and the Center for Naval Analyses, as well as the interagency evaluation conducted by the DoD and DoS Inspectors General. However, OUSD(P), DSCA, congressional, and COCOM representatives noted that most of the published reports focus on a small number of high-profile projects in Lebanon, Pakistan, Sierra Leone, and Yemen and thus do not constitute a program-wide assessment. Similarly, congressional reports provide snap assessments and anecdotal information, but they are based on qualitative observations rather than persistent data collection.

Stakeholders recognized that establishing a comprehensive assessment structure would be a complex process. They noted that assessments need to achieve several objectives:

- to measure the success of the 1206 Program authority in achieving national security priorities
- to assess the quality and timeliness of the implementation and execution of 1206 Program processes and activities
- to measure the impact of the individual projects that make up the larger authority.

Such an assessment would require input from all stakeholders, as well as formal guidance on objectives, assessment roles, data collection, and coordination between agencies.

Measurable Objectives Are Required on Multiple Levels

A number of stakeholders commented on the complexity involved in creating metrics for success for the 1206 Program. COCOM, congressional, OUSD(P), and DSCA representatives pointed out the inherent difficulty of measuring the success of counterterrorism measures, which are largely preventative actions. COCOM stakeholders also mentioned that there may be barriers to tracking partner-nation activity (including partner-nation secrecy), as well as in evaluating the sustainability and long-term strategic impact of specific 1206 Program projects. Many therefore observed that measures of effectiveness would need to be tailored to each stakeholder engaged in the different stages of the 1206 Program, and they offered a number of suggestions for the various types of objectives that might be included in future assessments. Such suggestions included counting the number of engagements in which a particular 1206 Program–funded capability is employed, evaluating whether a country is willing to accept additional training, and determining the extent to which an urgent or emergent threat to the United States has been addressed.

Stakeholders from OUSD(P), DSCA, the COCOMs, and the services provided examples of baseline data that would be required to determine whether the program is meeting its immediate goals. Sources included checklists as to timeliness and quality of equipment delivered or training executed, as well as reviews to determine whether partners are using the equipment and training for their intended purpose and how often (for example, the frequency of use of specific equipment against a target or whether the partner nation has used its new competency in counterterrorism missions). In some cases, it might be possible to measure the number of "bad guys" killed or captured, the number of terrorist operations disrupted, or the number of weapons caches recovered. In the case of training for stability operations, it would be possible to determine whether a partner nation was able to deploy on time as planned and whether it used its new competency during that deployment. For specific missions or skills, such as improvised explosive device detection or forensic exploitation, it could be possible to track the number of missions from which the team returned without any casualties.

Some COCOM stakeholders noted that obtaining data on partner-nation military activities can be difficult in regions in which U.S. forces are not engaged (and therefore do not have visibility in the field) or where local sovereignty is contested. It is often difficult, for example, to determine how a nation is using radar equipment provided by the United States or whether that radar contributes to counterterrorism missions.

Stakeholders also provided suggestions for measuring the indirect effects of the train and equip program, such as whether a partner nation is more willing to engage with the United

States as a result of participation in the 1206 Program or whether its operational relationship with the United States has improved. This could be determined by evaluating whether a country has become more willing to accept training or conduct U.S.-supported counterterrorism or stability operations because of participation in the 1206 Program. Stakeholders commented that such information is not easy to track or quantify. One can measure longer-term impacts by the extent to which a partner nation is willing to sustain its new capabilities (as demonstrated by committing its own funds for maintenance and spare parts, for example) and the extent to which 1206 Program–funded equipment or training is integrated into a partner nation's military force.

Some stakeholders commented on the importance of considering whether a partner nation has adjusted its doctrine to include the related mission. One COCOM representative suggested evaluating 1206 Program projects on how well they integrate with other security assistance and development efforts undertaken by DoD, DoS, and nongovernmental organizations. Many stakeholders suggested that strategic-level measures be included, such as the extent to which 1206 Program projects address urgent or emergent threats identified in the program submissions. For example, "Has a fire been put out?" "Has there been a reduction in the operating space of a threat?" "Has there has been a strategic shift as a result of the 1206 Program project?" We assert that these examples would also be notably difficult to quantify and to apply consistently across geographic regions.

1206 Program Assessment Roles and Responsibilities Will Require Clarification

Some of the informal assessment mechanisms that have been developed by the various offices engaged in 1206 Program projects could form the basis for a robust assessment process. Stakeholders indicated the potential utility of using existing data on proposal tracking, project milestones, equipment deliveries, and partner-nation capabilities in support of a more formal, program-wide assessment. However, the roles and responsibilities for these assessments would need to be expanded and defined more clearly.

Stakeholders across all offices recognized the need for comprehensive, program-wide assessments, yet nearly all of those interviewed expressed a concern about the lack of time available to assume the new responsibilities that such an assessment might require. The implementation of the 1206 Program itself has created additional work for security assistance officers, and assessments, in particular, take a great deal of time.

OUSD(P), DSCA, service, and COCOM representatives commented that any new assessment responsibilities given to current stakeholders would need to be sufficiently flexible to avoid generating additional stress for the staff involved. Although some stakeholders indicated that the COCOMs and country teams would have a primary role in conducting individual project assessments, most agreed that the responsibility for strategic assessment should be widely shared among the various offices engaged in the program.

Several stakeholders also expressed concern about the lack of training in either current procedures or a future assessment process. OUSD(P), DSCA, and service stakeholders, in particular, commented that few of those engaged in train and equip programs had specific training in security assistance or assessment processes, while others indicated that any future assessment responsibilities would require additional personnel training.

New Data Collection and Reporting Requirements Are Needed

Stakeholders acknowledged that new guidelines on data collection and reporting requirements would be necessary to begin conducting a more comprehensive program assessment. Noting that although current data collection occurs on an ad hoc basis, OUSD(P), DSCA, the COCOMs, and country team officials do collect data regularly. A number of stakeholders also mentioned the importance of developing a means of capturing the anecdotal information obtained in the field. Although anecdotes are not easily quantifiable, such information is critical to assessing partner-nation capabilities and willingness to engage in counterterrorism and stability operations. COCOM, DoS, congressional, OUSD(P), and DSCA stakeholders also emphasized the need to maintain consistent data collection structures over the course of several years to determine the long-term impact of 1206 Program projects. They stated that new reporting requirements would be necessary to ensure the sharing of data between agencies in a timely manner.

Improving Coordination with Key Agencies Is Critical

The creation of a consistent feedback loop would be helpful in implementing an effective assessment process, and stakeholders noted the need to improve information flows between agencies. One stakeholder commented that "inefficient feedback loops perpetuate information asymmetry." Providing a means for sharing data on a regular and timely basis would not only allow improve the quality of program assessments but would ultimately enhance program planning and execution.

Conclusion

In conducting the stakeholder interviews, the research team's intent was to gain a baseline understanding of the 1206 Program to facilitate the design of a formal survey to identify potential sources of data and potential assessors. The interviews with stakeholders were incredibly beneficial in clarifying the 1206 Program's current implementation processes and in identifying areas in which stakeholder views on the program differ. Indeed, the results of the formal survey, described in Chapter Four, elaborate on many of the issues raised here, particularly concerns about how a future assessment process would be incorporated into current staff responsibilities. Although the stakeholders interviewed held varying opinions about the design and implementation of the 1206 Program, all agreed that there is a need for a comprehensive assessment process.

The next chapter explores the survey responses with regard to data collection and potential roles and responsibilities for assessors.

CHAPTER FOUR

Applying the Framework to the 1206 Program: Results of the Survey

Every security cooperation program has multiple stakeholders, often scattered across multiple organizations at different levels and with different priorities and perspectives. In the case of the 1206 Program, we characterize the primary stakeholders as belonging to one of three levels: OSD (including DSCA), COCOM, or the services. Within OSD, one finds overall policy development and program management. While the focal point at this level is the OASD(SO/LIC&IC) 1206 Program team, DSCA also plays a key role in implementing the program. At the COCOM level, COCOM planners and country-specific security cooperation officers design and implement 1206 Program projects and activities. Finally, at the service level, security assistance agencies, such as the Air Force Security Assistance Center, and headquarters planners oversee acquisition and training associated with the projects. Non-DoD stakeholders may also have information about 1206 Program projects and sometimes even participate in activities or provide other resources that contribute to the overall program.

To understand the roles that these various stakeholders play in the 1206 Program and, more importantly, what roles they could play in project assessments, the RAND study team collected information from stakeholder representatives through an online survey conducted in August 2010. The survey was designed to gain specific insights into current and potential assessment capabilities.

This chapter begins by describing the analytical approach used by the RAND team to gather and examine information regarding 1206 Program assessments. Then, it presents a set of overall findings and concludes with a discussion of the implications for 1206 Program assessments.

Survey of 1206 Program Experts

The team used two separate approaches to ascertain the extent to which the security cooperation assessment approach detailed in previous work for the Air Force and for OUSD(P) was feasible for employment by the 1206 Program community. In addition to the interviews described in Chapter Three, the team conducted quantitative supporting analyses based on aggregate responses to a structured survey, titled "Section 1206 Global Train and Equip Request for Expert Feedback." (The survey is reproduced in full in the Appendix A.)

Constructing the Survey

Developing a survey that could elicit data from real stakeholders required the study team to move from the abstract nature of the evaluation hierarchy to a more concrete framework that described the program's essential parts and their relationships. To do this, the study team drew on a previously developed RAND approach, which addressed the assessment of Air Force security cooperation programs.[1] This approach resulted in a survey that asked questions about current program tasks, as opposed to theoretical assessment tasks. In addition, our survey drew on 1206 Program guidance and insights gained from interviews with various stakeholders as a way to ensure that the terminology was familiar to the respondents.

The survey questions were grouped into four broad areas—derived from and connected to the hierarchy of evaluation—in which a stakeholder might be involved:

- *Process Implementation.* Some stakeholders carry out specific tasks as assigned by program managers. These tasks might include organizing an event or providing subject-matter expertise, establishing contracts, accounting for funds, or processing documentation required by Air Force instructions or other directives.
- *Process Design and Development.* Other stakeholders participate in the design or development of processes, carrying out such activities as developing lesson plans, contracts, or event agendas.
- *Program Recommendations.* Some stakeholders make recommendations to program managers about the size of, scope of, or need for the program or a specific activity.
- *Program Decisions.* Still other stakeholders make decisions regarding specific activities, the need for, or the scope of the program.

Questions in each category allowed us to categorize respondents and connect survey responses back to the broader assessment framework. The survey employed terms and references that were familiar to the respondents and asked concrete questions about the activities in which the respondents were currently engaged.

By mapping the answers back to assessment roles, we identified where there was potential for assessment capability and where there were possible gaps. We then developed insights to inform OUSD(P) efforts to implement a comprehensive assessment framework, as described in this report.

We also reviewed guidance documents to identify the types of documentation and data collection required for specific 1206 Program projects. Table 4.1 shows the types of data that could be collected and assessed across an entire program. The documents listed in the table were either specifically cited in OUSD(P) guidance or mentioned by stakeholders during our interviews.

We approached the construction of these questions with the understanding that program guidance forms the basis for assessment. In other words, program guidance documents the need for a program and its objectives and often tells program managers how to design and implement their programs. Although OUSD(P) publishes formal program guidelines and lessons learned, which are distributed formally though the Joint Staff to the COCOMs, not everyone in the 1206 Program stakeholder community is aware of this guidance. Stakeholders are familiar with emailed instructions from OUSD(P), however. Without formal guidance

---

[1]   See Moroney, Hogler, et al., 2010, and Marquis, Hogler, et al., 2010.

Table 4.1
Types of 1206 Program Data That Can Be Collected, by Topic

Topic	Type of Data		
Demand	Acquisition of equipment, supplies, or spares	Discussions with country team members	Project proposal
	Section 1206 Program proposal	Exchange agreement	Proposal development
	After-action reports	Intelligence sources	Quality assurance reports
	Background material	International agreements	Reports to Congress
	Bills of lading or other receipts for the delivery of goods	Lesson plans or other training material	Request for disclosure authorization
	Briefings	Letter of request/letter of acceptance	Request for fund cite
	Budget allocation memo	Master data agreement	Requirements or proposal prioritization document
	Budget projection	Meeting or conference agenda	Security plan
	Budget request	Memorandum of agreement	Site survey reports
	Contract award	Memorandum of understanding	Status, update, IPR, or similar briefings
	Contract performance	Own observations/trip report	Training quotas
	Contract preparation	Participant entry or exit testing	Training reports
	Country desk officers	Project agreement/ arrangement memos	Travel orders
	Discussion with partner-nation representatives		U.S. military trainers
			Visit request
Resources	Acquisition of equipment, supplies, or spares	Contract preparation	Proposal development
	Section 1206 Program proposal	Lesson plans or other training material	Request for disclosure authorization
	Background material	Letter of request/letter of acceptance	Request for fund cite
	Briefings	Master data agreement	Requirements or proposal prioritization document
	Budget allocation memo	Meeting or conference agenda	Security plan
	Budget projection	Project proposal	Site survey
	Budget request		Visit request
Costs	319 funds transfer	Loan agreement	Releasability request
	After-action reports	Monthly report	Reports to Congress
	Annual report	Own observations/trip report	Request for fund cite
	Budget allocation memo	Periodic financial report	Requirements or proposal prioritization document
	Budget projection	Program proposal	Status, update, or IPR report
	Budget request	Programmatic review	Test and disposition report
	Embassy concurrent cable	Progress report	Training report
	FAA Section 505 agreement	Project final report	Travel orders
	Financial reports	Quality assurance report	Travel vouchers
	Human rights vetting request	Quarterly obligation report	

Table 4.1—Continued

Topic	Type of Data		
Objectives	After-action reports	FAA Section 505 agreement	Project quarterly report
	Annual report	Financial reports	Quality assurance report
	Certification to Congress	Guest lists	Quarterly obligation report
	Conference, subject-matter expert exchange, or roundtable discussion	Human rights vetting request	Quid pro quo analysis
		Informal discussions	Releasability request
	Contract award	Information exchange agreement	Reports to Congress
	Contract performance	Interim tour report	Request for foreign disclosure authorization
	Data exchange annex	International visit request	Request for human rights vetting
	Delegation of disclosure authority letter	Letter of acceptance	
	Delivery of equipment	Letter of request	Requirements or proposal prioritization document
	Discussion with country desk officers	Meeting minutes/summary	Security plan
		Monthly report	Status, update, or IPR briefing
	Discussion with partner-nation representatives	Own observations/trip report	Test and disposition report
		Nomination package	Training quotas
	Embassy concurrent cable	Program proposal	Training report
	End-of-tour report	Programmatic review	Travel orders or invitational travel orders
	Equipment installation	Progress report	
	Extended visit authorization	Project final report	Trip report
			Visit request

NOTE: FAA = Foreign Assistance Act. IPR = interim progress review.

regarding data collection and assessment, we relied on the results of discussions with 1206 Program managers and other stakeholders to develop the set of potential data sources.

1206 Program Guidance

While OUSD(P) and DSCA do provide guidance, it is often supplemented by stakeholders' organizational handbooks, checklists, operating instructions, and other documents that capture local procedures and ensure continuity as programs change hands. COCOM project managers and service-level stakeholders may, because of their close proximity to project activities and events, have much greater insight into a program's true workings than is outlined in top-level guidance.

This collective body of documentation, both formal and informal, forms a more complete source for both data collection and assessment of 1206 Program project-level activities, and, as such, it is important to understand what it comprises and how extensive it is.

We asked survey respondents to comment on the availability of guidance documents, as well as to describe the documents that they develop themselves. We asked respondents specifically about formal guidance, as well as internal operating procedures and other program-specific documents that would guide the conduct of the program.

Survey Respondents

In close collaboration with the study sponsor, the RAND team identified key 1206 Program stakeholders who would be invited to take the survey. Approximately 40 percent of the invited participants submitted surveys pertaining to 1206 Program projects. Specifically, 56 of

136 identified stakeholders responded, a very strong response rate for a survey of this kind.[2] In addition, each of the three organizational levels (OSD, DSCA, the COCOMs, and the services) are represented.

Responses reported here are not attributed to specific offices or individuals. Instead, as in Chapter Three, we grouped the survey respondents according to three levels: (1) OSD/DSCA, (2) COCOM, and (3) service. By grouping the respondents in this way, we were able to maintain the respondent's privacy while gaining insight into potential 1206 Program assessment roles and an understanding of where gaps might exist.

Findings and Observations

Many stakeholders plan, implement, and generally support 1206 Program projects, each contributing to the program's effectiveness. By analyzing the results of the survey, we identified key areas to help strengthen the ability of OUSD(P) to assess its security cooperation programs. In this section, we describe these key areas and provide detailed examples that give insight into current gaps.

Formal Guidance on the Assessment Process Is Needed

Among other things, assessment at all levels requires clearly articulated objectives; without formal guidance to lay out objectives, roles and responsibilities, and reporting requirements, it will be very difficult to effectively assess the 1206 Program. The 1206 Program suffers from a perception that it is a transient initiative, which may stem from its year-to-year continuation in legislation as opposed to status as an established program of record. The short-term, gap-filling focus of the program also contributes to this perception.

The purpose of the 1206 Program is both building partnership capacity and facilitating the conduct of counterterrorism and stability operations. About half of our survey respondents saw building partner capacity as the program's primary end state, while the other half emphasized the counterterrorism mission as the program's overall goal. It would be helpful to reconcile these differing ideas about priorities, sustainability, and success prior to assessment, and the most effective mechanism for doing so will likely be formal guidance.

Another issue that stems from the lack of formal guidance is the disconnect between setting objectives and designing projects. Table 4.2 illustrates this problem. Despite a large number of respondents claiming that they design projects and activities, a remarkably small number admitted to setting objectives.

This finding raises questions about the basis on which project designers are developing project proposals. The data suggest that OUSD(P) and DSCA are not predefining the objectives for the COCOMs, yet the COCOMs do not appear to be defining the objectives either. In the best case, as addressed in the next section, the process is simply somewhat opaque. In the worst case, there are no clear objectives being set. In either case, clear, formal guidance can help alleviate this problem.

---

[2]   See Matthias Schonlau, Ronald D. Fricker, and Marc N. Elliott, *Conducting Research Surveys via E-Mail and the Web*, Santa Monica, Calif.: RAND Corporation, MR-1480-RC, 2002.

Table 4.2
Disconnects Between Setting Objectives and Program Design

Question	Percentage of Survey Respondents		
	OSD/DSCA	COCOMs	Services
16. Do you design specific events or activities for this Section 1206 project?	38	41	25
28. Do you set the objectives for the specific projects?	0	12	4
29. Do you set the objectives for specific events or activities within specific projects?	0	6	4

Measurable Objectives That Explicitly Connect to Broader U.S. Government, Theater, Regional, and 1206 Project Goals Are Lacking

Individual 1206 Program projects are connected to regional end states under GEF, COCOM TCPs, and each embassy's mission strategic resource plan. Country teams are required to justify these connections on the program proposal form.

However, based on survey results, there appeared to be some disconnect among the survey respondents about the connection between individual programs and higher-level guidance. There also appeared to be confusion among the survey respondents about who was responsible for setting objectives for individual projects. The proposal template requires the country teams to include the project's objective (the capability shortfall to be addressed). As described earlier, the least frequently cited activity conducted by survey respondents was "setting objectives for projects or specific activities." Between 0 and 12 percent of respondents claimed that they set objectives for individual projects, and only between 0 and 6 percent set such objectives for activities that were conducted in support of the projects. Without identifying a clear source of project and activity objectives, it is difficult to assign responsibility for project and activity assessment, let alone overall program assessment. We see a manifestation of this in the number of respondents who claimed to collect data regarding how well the projects were meeting objectives. Table 4.3 illustrates this point, indicating that one-fourth to nearly two-fifths of respondents stated that they gathered such data.

Not understanding where objectives are being set simply raises speculation. Since substantial numbers of respondents indicated that they did in fact design programs, one conclusion might be that project objectives are being drawn from other guidance documents, such as the GEF, COCOM plans and strategies, or other, perhaps service-level, strategies. This would be the best case. On the other hand, it is not possible to confirm this assumption based on the survey results.

Table 4.3
Disconnects Between Setting Objectives and Collecting Data on Their Achievement

Question	Percentage of Survey Respondents		
	OSD/DSCA	COCOMs	Services
25. Do you gather data that reflect how well a specific event or activity met its objectives?	38	24	32
28. Do you set the objectives for the specific projects?	0	12	4
29. Do you set the objectives for specific events or activities within specific projects?	0	6	4

Gaps Exist in Data Collection and Reporting Requirements

One of the more revealing results from the survey was that the most common data source cited by respondents, regardless of the type of data collected, was "my own observations." Stakeholders who directly observe activities and events tend to be in the best position to collect the data that will be used for assessments. It can be problematic, however, when simple observations replace formal mechanisms for collecting and routing data. In the case of the 1206 Program, it appears that data collection is mostly informal, although formal mechanisms do exist for many of the routine procedural aspects, such as budgeting, contracting, and acquisition activities. Table 4.4 presents seven questions that helped clarify the types of data collected, as well as the stakeholder levels that collect them.

One observation from Table 4.4 is that data collection appears to be spread out across a large number of organizations; the relatively low percentages of respondents collecting data, along with their consistency across stakeholder levels, suggests that no single office is collecting all of the data needed to conduct assessments. Two particularly noteworthy findings shown in the table reveal gaps resulting from the short-term focus of the program, as discussed earlier.

First, visibility at all levels tends to focus on day-to-day processing and implementation rather than long-term objectives or outcomes. Services, for example, appear focused on routine implementation (i.e., the FMS process), while higher levels focus on meeting administrative deadlines. Question 7, for example, had a relatively high positive response rate compared with those of all the other data collection questions, ranging from 50 to 61 percent. This question, however, has to do with data regarding timeliness and accuracy, as well as appropriateness. Timeliness and accuracy are clearly short-term output objectives, and while important from a management standpoint, they reveal little about the overall effect of the program. Similarly, data regarding legal compliance is essential, but they do little to help the program manager understand the extent to which program objectives are being met.

Second, the least understood aspects of the program included partner views, effects on partner capabilities, and the appropriateness of partner representatives participating in 1206

Table 4.4
Types of Assessment Data Collected by Survey Respondents

Question	Percentage of Survey Respondents		
	OSD/DSCA	COCOMs	Services
7. Do you collect data regarding the timeliness, accuracy, or appropriateness of the assistance provided to partner nation(s)?	50	59	61
9. Do you collect data regarding participant views or observations, such as exit surveys?	13	24	11
10. Do you collect data regarding capabilities assessments?	13	47	25
11. Do you collect data regarding the effect of the 1206 project on relevant partner capabilities?	25	47	7
12. Do you collect data regarding the funds expended?	50	29	46
13. Do you collect data regarding compliance with legal or regulatory requirements related to the project?	25	29	25
21. Do you collect data regarding the cost of the overall project or the cost of a unit of output (i.e., one graduate, one event, etc.)?	25	18	11

Program project-level activities.[3] In particular, according to the survey results, partner-nation views were not well understood. However, such an understanding is critical to determining assessment roles and responsibilities. Stakeholders at the COCOM level routinely interact with partners and will likely be in the best position to collect such data.

To illustrate the divide between data related to short-term administrative issues and the longer-term achievement of objectives, Figures 4.1 and 4.2 depict sources used in collecting outcome assessment data and process and implementation assessment data, respectively. There is, of course, considerable overlap between the questions asked for each assessment level; as one in a series of nested assessments, each level draws from and builds on the preceding levels. To isolate the unique data sources used in each type of assessment, however, the study team identified the survey questions pertaining each. Three questions were directly relevant to process and implementation assessments:

- Question 7: Do you collect data regarding the timeliness, accuracy, or appropriateness of the assistance provided to partner nation(s)?
- Question 8: Do you collect data regarding partner-nation representatives such as attendees, participants, recipients, or numbers of individuals trained?
- Question 13: Do you collect data regarding compliance with legal or regulatory requirements related to the project?

Each of these questions is also indirectly relevant to outcome assessments, when aggregated over time. But the team also found that three questions were of immediate relevance to outcome assessments:

- Question 9: Do you collect data regarding participant views or observations, such as exit surveys?
- Question 10: Do you collect data regarding capabilities assessments?
- Question 11: Do you collect data regarding the effect of the 1206 project on relevant partner capabilities?

Process and implementation assessments had the widest range of data sources of any assessment level, with 20 separate data sources identified by respondents (as shown in Figure 4.1). Of the 56 survey respondents, 34—or more than 60 percent—indicated that they collected this type of information already.

Less well sourced were data regarding long-range outcomes, with only ten sources identified by respondents (as shown in Figure 4.2). Moreover, the actual collection of this type of data was much more limited than that for process and implementation. For example, of the 56 respondents, only 19—or just over one-third—indicated that they collected this type of data. Of the 34 respondents who were collecting process and implementation data, just over half (55 percent) were also collecting outcome data.

This suggests an issue that may hinder the effectiveness of assessments at both the outcome and cost-effectiveness levels. Without adequate collection of data regarding the achievement of outcome objectives, cost-effectiveness assessments, which rely on the results of each of

---

[3]   We are referring to partner-nation representatives participating in project-level activities that occur after the project has been approved and implemented. In other words, "Is the partner nation sending the right people for training?"

the other levels (because of the nested nature of the assessment hierarchy) will be difficult to conduct and will yield questionable results.

Figure 4.1
Data Sources Identified for Process and Implementation Assessments

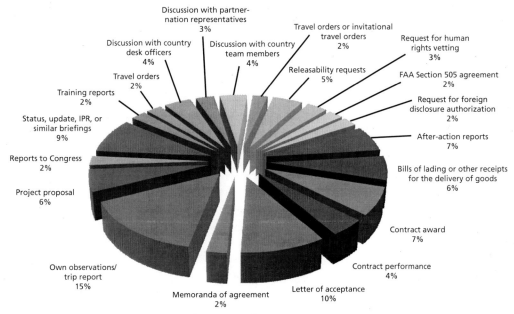

NOTE: Percentages do not sum to 100 due to rounding.
RAND *TR1121-4.1*

Figure 4.2
Data Sources Identified for Outcome Assessments

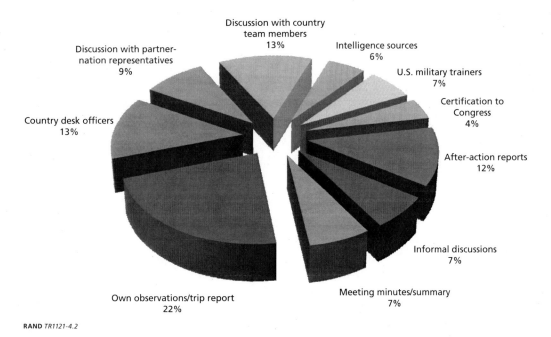

RAND *TR1121-4.2*

1206 Program Assessment Roles and Responsibilities Are Currently Unclear

Many of the comments in response to the open-ended question, "Please share with us any additional information you believe is pertinent to our inquiry or any comments you have about the instrument or our research," dealt with communication between organizations involved with the 1206 Program. As one respondent stated, "I think it is very important to involve the right people in the beginning of the process." To do this, it must first be clear who the "right people" are in the context of conducting assessments.

As described in Chapter Two, there are five levels of assessments, and for each level to be operationalized into actual assessments, both data collectors and assessors must be identified. A key principle that guides the identification of data collectors and assessors is that they must be in a position to collect or assess the data, respectively. Clearly, with so many data sources, each assessment will have multiple data collectors. But the unique data requirements of the five levels suggest that the data collectors at one assessment level may be different from data collectors at other levels. Because the data reside far and wide, so do the data collectors, and without clear guidance regarding roles and responsibilities, some data may not be collected or may simply not be routed to the appropriate collector. The same logic holds true for assessors.

In a complex program like 1206, expecting one office or stakeholder to conduct all the assessments may be unrealistic. For example, the services may be well positioned to assess the effectiveness of the acquisition processes, while the COCOMs may be in a good position to assess the appropriateness of the systems delivered or the capacity that a project builds. OUSD(P) and DSCA may be positioned to assess the achievement of outcomes. In each case, designating a single office in each stakeholder organization to coordinate data collection and assessment responsibilities will serve to eliminate some of the complexity. Drawing on the data gathered during this study from both the survey and the interviews will simplify the assignment of the roles and responsibilities for assessments.

Limited Insight into Other DoD Programs May Hinder Cost-Effectiveness Assessments

Understanding the objectives and priorities attached to other, similar DoD security cooperation programs is essential for conducting assessments of cost-effectiveness. As described earlier, survey respondents generally had limited insight into other programs.

At the service level, only 7 percent of respondents indicated that they had access to information regarding other DoD security cooperation programs. This, in itself, may not pose a challenge for 1206 Program assessments, as the types of information the survey asked about had to do with other programs' objectives, costs, and priority within DoD. Service-level respondents typically worked on issues related to acquisition processes and were not necessarily involved in the policy associated with individual programs. However, at the OSD and COCOM levels, where one might expect a greater breadth of knowledge regarding other security cooperation programs, only about 40 percent of the respondents professed such knowledge.

Limited insight into other DoD programs may hinder cost-effectiveness and program assessments, as this type of information is essential for the comparative analysis that these assessments draw on. There are, in fact, numerous sources of data regarding DoD security cooperation programs—and the problem may be that there are too many. When asked where they derive their information regarding security cooperation programs, those respondents who could answer reported that they collectively identified no fewer than 20 sources, ranging from discussions with desk officers to electronic databases and websites, of which seven were cited.

The lack of a single source of information may make it difficult for stakeholders to access the information they need.

Respondents Were Not Always Aware of Guidance

The survey asked each survey respondent to answer three questions related to guidance for program design and the development of project activities. The first queried whether there were DoD instructions (DoDIs), manuals, or other directives. Although OUSD(P) publishes annual formal program guidelines and lessons learned, less than one-third of respondents knew about them. At the OUSD(P)/DSCA level, 25 percent said "yes," while at the COCOM level, 18 percent said "yes." At the service level, 40 percent said "yes" but primarily cited FMS process-oriented documents, such as the *Security Assistance Management Manual* and Air Force Instruction 16-101.[4] Perhaps reassuringly, many cited the DSCA memo "Guidance for Development of FY09 Section 1206 Programs."[5] Interestingly, only 14 percent of respondents were aware of any non-DoD guidance. Among those who were aware, the mostly commonly cited guidance included DoS cables, the FAA regulations, NDAA, embassy mission strategic resource plans, and presidential directives.

Stakeholders Create Their Own Guidance in the Absence of Formal Guidance

Finally, the survey asked respondents whether they used informal guidance documents, such as continuity binders, to aid in the design and development of programs. As might be expected, a substantial number of respondents indicated such use. Slightly less than 20 percent of the respondents indicated they used informal guidance sources, primarily email, informal discussions, internally prepared documents, and websites.

Assessment Skills Exist but Could Be Improved

To gain insight into the respondents' views of their ability to conduct actual assessments, we asked about the skills they possess that could enable them to conduct such assessments. Respondents were asked to comment on existing assessment skills that they, or their successors, might bring to the job, as well as their view of the need for assessment skills training, checklists, and instructions on how to accomplish assessments.

The first of three questions asked respondents to comment on the skills that they believed they already possessed. Specifically, they were asked, "Do you believe that you, or personnel assigned to your position in the future, have/will have the skills to conduct appropriate security cooperation assessments (e.g., regarding the need for a program, program design, program compliance with policy, program outcomes, and program cost-effectiveness)?" Overall, slightly less than one-third answered "yes," suggesting that these skills are generally lacking among those involved with the 1206 Program.

To understand what it might take to prepare a potential assessor to conduct assessments, the survey asked respondents, "If no, do you believe that you, or personnel assigned to your position in the future, would be prepared to conduct assessments if you had an appropriate

---

[4] Defense Security Cooperation Agency, *Security Assistance Management Manual*, Washington, D.C., DoD 5105.38M, October 3, 2003; Air Force Instruction 16-101, International Affairs and Security Assistance Management, February 15, 2011.

[5] Defense Security Cooperation Agency, "Guidance for Development of FY09 Section 1206 Programs," memorandum, February 3, 2009.

checklist and set of instructions?" Only a quarter of those who had answered "no" to the first question answered "yes" to this question, suggesting that developing an assessment instruction and accompanying assessment checklists may not be an effective way to prepare those involved with 1206 Program projects to conduct assessments of them or that they may simply be insufficient on their own. Finally, respondents who answered "no" to both of the first two questions (in other words, those who did not believe that they had the skills and also did not believe that an instruction or checklist would help) were asked a third question: "If no, do you believe that completion of a short course on conducting assessments (via classroom or online instruction) would be adequate preparation for someone in your position?" About 25 percent of these respondents answered positively, implying that there might be a marginal additional value in creating classes or other training for assessments. These two measures may have a cumulative effect that could help ensure that stakeholders do have the necessary skills.

Conclusions

In general, the analysis suggests that there are stakeholders throughout DoD who have the potential to both collect data and assess the 1206 Program. While only one-third believed that they currently had the skills to conduct these assessments, another third believed that they could become capable of doing so through either additional training or the right instructions and checklists.

Data sources are available to support each type of assessment, and although these sources are fragmented and widely dispersed, at least some respondents were already collecting and using such data. Additionally, the stakeholder responses suggest that appropriate assessors may be found, but it is not likely that they will be in one office or even at one stakeholder level.

There are other impediments to implementing an effective assessment program. Clear and consistent assessment guidance needs to be developed and disseminated. In particular, potential data collectors and assessors need to be aware of overall program and individual activity objectives, an issue that is closely tied to clearly defined roles and responsibilities. The survey highlighted that improvements are needed in terms of stakeholder coordination and information sharing, particularly across programs. In addition, reporting requirements, if they exist, may not be fully understood or met. Furthermore, clear program advocates with the right authority to set objectives are essential for implementing the assessment framework. The next chapter examines these findings and offers conclusions and recommendations for 1206 Program managers.

CHAPTER FIVE

Conclusions and Recommendations

Assessments in the security cooperation business are not easy. Security cooperation activities with partner nations take place at many levels, over multiple years, with varying purposes. The transient nature of these interactions makes qualitative, longer-term outcomes difficult to discern.

Chapter One identified some of the key challenges associated with security cooperation assessments, including a lack of specific guidance and assessment frameworks from OUSD(P) and the COCOMs, the difficulty of achieving objectivity in data collection and analysis, the longer-term nature of assessing outcomes (rather than inputs and outputs of particular events), and the necessary training of individuals to conduct such assessments, to name a few. This report provided specific examples in the context of interviews and survey results to illustrate how these challenges affect the 1206 Program.

However, as both the interviews and the survey indicated, 1206 Program stakeholders support the idea of instituting a comprehensive assessment framework. All seemed to recognize that, while difficult, qualitative assessments provide valuable information about the success of a particular activity and, if completed thoughtfully and correctly, can help stakeholders identify lessons and possible best practices. One of the most important aspects to keep in mind is the need to set *specific, measureable objectives* for program activities. In the case of the 1206 Program, this refers specifically to the project level, where set objectives are not currently in place. While project objectives are included in individual program proposals, many of the project objectives are not very specific or measurable. Moreover, under the current assessment approach, the focus tends to be on assessing inputs expended (e.g., funding, manpower) rather than on outcomes.

Importantly, as stated throughout this report, the purpose of conducting security cooperation assessments, or any kind of assessments for that matter, is to inform decisionmaking at many levels—policy, program manager, and execution—as well as to inform the planning and resource allocation processes. This requires an assessment framework that includes clear guidance, measureable objectives, indicators and metrics attached to those objectives, trained data collectors and assessors, and dedicated resources.

This report lays the groundwork for a comprehensive assessment framework for the 1206 Program. Our approach takes a longer-term view, with the understanding that accurate assessments, especially when measuring outcomes and cost-effectiveness, take time and effort. However, laying the groundwork now will enable quicker results.

This chapter is divided into three sections. The first presents key findings from the research effort, summarizing from Chapters Three and Four, in particular. The second section provides specific, actionable recommendations that are linked to the key findings. The third section describes an implementation plan for assessing the 1206 Program over time relative to the key insights that were introduced in Chapter One.

Findings

The study team identified five key findings over the course of this research effort. First, we found that the 1206 Program lacks formal guidance for an assessment process. Such guidance would help all 1206 stakeholders understand the importance of comprehensive assessment for program effectiveness and that assessment is a goal of OUSD(P). The guidance should include clearly articulated and measurable objectives at the program level. Differing ideas regarding priorities, sustainability of 1206 Program projects, and "success" must first be reconciled for assessment to serve policy goals. Finally, such guidance would articulate the need for specificity in project requests (i.e., requesting capabilities such as "radar" is unhelpful without additional details and holds up the process).

Second, measurable objectives at the project level are essential to assessing overall outcomes. According to our survey data, setting objectives for projects or specific activities is the least frequently cited activity conducted by 1206 Program stakeholders (i.e., 0–12 percent for projects, 0–6 percent for activities). Despite developing and implementing proposals, COCOMs and service staffs have limited insight into how projects meet 1206 Program objectives, let alone broader effects and unintended consequences. There appears to be a disconnect between setting objectives, understanding partner views, and collecting data on "timeliness and accuracy." Such results suggest that the current focus is on meeting proposal and funding deadlines rather than setting objectives and implementing an effective project.

A third key finding is that gaps seem to exist in the data collection and reporting requirements process. According to the survey results, the most common data source was "my own observations," often accounting for more than one-fifth of the responses. Moreover, data collection efforts appear to be spread across a large number of organizations. Assessments at the process and implementation level seem to have the widest range of data sources. Overall, however, data are not reaching those stakeholders charged with conducting assessments. It is very important to note that there tends to be greater visibility at all levels in terms of day-to-day implementation rather than long-term objectives or outcomes. For example, the military services appear focused on routine process and implementation-level tasks, while higher levels focus on administrative deadlines and reporting requirements. Finally, among the least understood aspects of the data collection process are partner views, effects on partner capabilities, and appropriateness of partner representatives.

The fourth finding is that 1206 Program assessment roles and responsibilities for stakeholders are currently unclear and unassigned. In short, those who may have the means to collect data or assess specific projects are not being tasked to do so. However, even if they were tasked at the COCOM and service headquarters level, the availability of experienced, trained manpower to do the job may be an issue. Day-to-day responsibilities for 1206 Program management at the headquarters level are a temporary duty. It is not possible to hire additional permanent staff because the program is an annual authority, subject to renewal or cancellation each year. Therefore, offices tend to focus intently on each new 1206 tranche four times throughout the course of the year, then scale back their efforts significantly. In short, with the exception of one COCOM, which has hired a contractor, the program does not receive full-time attention throughout the year at the COCOM level. Collecting data and assessing the 1206 Program's performance and impact are not presently a task at the field level.

The fifth finding is that OUSD(P) could improve coordination with key stakeholders, both within DoD and elsewhere—namely DoS and key congressional committees. After the approval of specific projects at the policy level, interview results suggest that there is limited transparency among stakeholders, making it difficult for OUSD(P) to track timelines and deliverables. Moreover, our interviewees relayed some concern expressed by congressional staffers regarding the perceived divergences between DoS and DoD on specific 1206 Program projects, particularly during the notification process.

Recommendations

The study team identified nine recommendations for OUSD(P)'s consideration that link to the key findings discussed in this chapter.

Recommendation 1: Develop an Implementation Plan for 1206 Program Assessments

OUSD(P) should consider developing an implementation plan to ensure the effective and efficient rollout of a new assessment framework for the 1206 Program. Included in the implementation plan should be near- and longer-term activities to ensure that a comprehensive assessment framework will be implemented in the future. The third section of this chapter describes the elements of an implementation plan in detail, focusing on a "two-track" approach to address immediate and longer-term assessment questions from multiple stakeholders.

Recommendation 2: Develop and Disseminate "Life-Cycle" Guidance for Project Development, Implementation, and Assessment

Disseminating the assessment guidance contained in the in-progress DoDI on the 1206 Program, if time allows before its release, is advisable. If time does not allow, OUSD(P) might follow up with an addendum that specifies the new process for assessing the 1206 Program, including resources and timelines for implementation.

Recommendation 3: Ensure That 1206 Program Stakeholders Understand Their Assessment Roles

OUSD(P) should ensure that all stakeholders associated with the 1206 Program, particularly the COCOMs and the military services, have a clear understanding of which data they are responsible for collecting, how 1206 Program assessment data should be stored, and to whom and how often they should be disseminated. This could also be addressed in the DoDI or in a follow-up addendum on assessments.

Recommendation 4: Establish a Process for Setting Objectives at the Project and Activity Levels

Currently, there is no process for setting and communicating objectives at the project and activity levels for the 1206 Program, which severely hinders OUSD(P)'s ability to assess the program in a comprehensive way. OUSD(P) should establish such a process and communicate it to those planning and executing 1206 Program projects, perhaps through the DoDI, emphasizing that specific, measureable objectives for each project are essential to the assessment process. It would be helpful to headquarters level staff as well as to those on the execution side in the field to provide some examples of measurable project objectives, perhaps from prior 1206 Program projects. In addition, a mechanism should be established to store and track project objectives for future reference.

Recommendation 5: Systematically Collect Data Regarding Achievement of Objectives and Consider Using Focus Groups to Develop Metrics

Assuming that project objectives are measureable (see recommendation 4), OUSD(P) should consider tasking those executing 1206 Program projects to collect specific data relative to each objective. These objectives should link to specific metrics. To develop the metrics, OUSD(P) could set up focus group sessions that include individuals involved in past 1206 Program projects. These groups could be capability-focused (e.g., maritime surveillance and interdiction, air mobility), but their job would be to establish benchmark metrics to enable future 1206 Program assessments at the project level, relative to specific capabilities.

Recommendation 6: Identify Data Collectors Based on Their Proximity to the Action

OUSD(P) should ensure that stakeholders are tasked with collecting 1206 project-level data for which they are actually responsible. A positive example of this would be to ask the Air Force Security Cooperation Center to collect data on acquisition costs and timeliness for an aviation system purchased under the 1206 Program. A negative example would be to ask the COCOM to do so instead. In other words, it is necessary for those charged with gathering data to be "near the action" that is the subject of the data. By this we mean subject-matter or functional experts engaged in the provision of 1206 Program assistance to partners. It is important to pass these data on to assessors, preferably at the COCOM level, before passing the results to OUSD(P) and DoS to be integrated with data from other programs at the policymaking level.

Recommendation 7: Host an Annual Conference of 1206 Program Stakeholders at the Policymaking Level

In addition to DSCA and COCOM 1206 Program conferences and teleconferences, which do not currently include stakeholders outside of DoD, OUSD(P) should consider holding an annual higher-level 1206 Program conference that includes DoD and DoS officials to review guidance and solicit discussion on program improvement and assessment. Individual meetings with key senior-level stakeholders at the COCOMs and services are another possibility, but the conference itself would provide a needed venue for senior policymakers in the 1206 Program community to benefit from collective discussion.

Recommendation 8: Consider Developing an Automated Tool to Facilitate the Collection and Reporting of Assessment Data

Building on the RAND team's 1206 Program assessment survey, OUSD(P) should consider developing a tool to serve as a repository for 1206 Program data and to facilitate program- and project-level assessments. The tool should be a modular template, with different components dictated by specific projects and data collector roles, sent out at certain intervals with automatic reminders. Such a tool would likely diminish the strain on overtasked action officers at the headquarters level who have been given 1206 Program responsibilities as an extra task. Action officers would be aware of the types of data needed to complete the templates and would receive reminders when they are due.

Recommendation 9: Consider Hiring Outside Support or Appointing Career Staff to Be "Program Representatives" at Each COCOM

Because the 1206 Program is not a permanent authority, the COCOMs have tasked 1206 Program management responsibilities as added duties for action officers, typically at the major or lieutenant colonel level. Our research indicates that additional support is needed for the implementation of an assessment framework for the 1206 Program. The program and its specific projects require full-time attention, especially at USEUCOM, USPACOM, and USCENTCOM, which presently carry out the majority of 1206 Program projects. We recommend that OUSD(P) consider hiring "program representatives" to support the respective COCOMs in managing and implementing the 1206 Program and that data collection for the assessment process be a primary responsibility of this individual or group. We suggest that these 1206 Program representatives should include one or two mid- to senior-level analysts, either as outside support or as one or two career staff. OUSD(P) might consider hiring a larger team of analysts on a case-by-case basis to conduct specific project-level assessments in key countries, but it is important to provide those data and findings to the permanent COCOM 1206 Program representative.

The Implemention Plan

This section presents an illustrative plan of action for implementing the preceding recommendations. Although we divide the plan into two tracks of near- and longer-term actions, several of the activities can be undertaken simultaneously as resources and time allow. Track 1 offers relatively low-cost steps that can be implemented in the short term, whereas track 2 comprises some longer-term, potentially more costly and time-consuming steps but ones that ultimately would provide a more solid basis for informal program decisions.

Using this two-track approach, the assessment implementation plan can guide OUSD(P)'s effort to establish a set of hierarchical assessments in support of the 1206 Program. Track 1 consists of near-term actions that can be quickly put into place for a limited assessment process, providing a quick look at the program's cost-effectiveness. It is important to caveat such an assessment by clarifying assumptions regarding the achievement of outcome and output objectives, but it still provides a useful comparison of the 1206 Program to other, similar security cooperation programs. Track 1 would use existing resources to collect data and conduct assessments and would serve to satisfy congressional demand for program assessment.

Track 1: Near-Term Actions

Track 1 comprises four key insights that flow from the findings described in Chapters Three and Four and is designed to implement the recommendations presented in this chapter.

Provide formal guidance on the assessment process. As described earlier, clear, formal guidance is essential and forms the foundation for developing a sound assessment program. Guidance must be timely, clear, and widely disseminated. As a minimum, it should identify sources of objectives (i.e., GEF, COCOM) and which stakeholders will be responsible for setting individual project and activity objectives. The guidance should describe the assessment process, step-by-step, and clearly identify timelines for conducting the assessments. Developing and publishing guidance is the first and perhaps most important step in establishing an effective assessment program. In addition to these specific entries, the guidance should, to the extent possible, include the other key insights in both track 1 and track 2.

Establish 1206 assessment roles and responsibilities. With the proper guidance in place, stakeholders' knowledge of their roles and responsibilities should be complete. Identifying specific roles in the program, such as data collector, assessor, reviewer, and integrator, is essential. Ensuring that the roles and responsibilities match up with capabilities and access to data is equally essential, and despite the degree of complexity, it adds to the overall management of the assessment program, and the results in terms of quality of data and assessment should make it worthwhile. In particular, the plan must consider the most appropriate roles and responsibilities for each level of assessment. Because of the fragmented nature of the program, the integrator role, most likely to be taken on by OUSD(P) with the support of DoS, will be particularly important. By gathering inputs, including a variety of individual assessments of specific aspects of the program, the integrator will be required to assemble a meaningful overall assessment of the program.

In addition to assigning roles and responsibilities, the plan should also consider offering specialized training for stakeholders charged with conducting the assessments. Finally, those in the position to do so should be responsible for obtaining partner country input and feedback on individual projects as an essential part of the assessment process.

Set data collection and reporting requirements. With clear roles and responsibilities defined, instituting repeatable processes to ensure that all stakeholders know which data to collect and where to send them will ensure that information flows from the proper sources to the right assessors in a consistent way over time. Whether the data consist of formal budget documents or anecdotal observations, knowing what to collect, where, when, and how will be essential. It is equally important to know to whom to pass the data.

The key to this information flow is to identify specific offices responsible for collecting certain types of data, based on the functions that they currently perform for the 1206 Program. It is important to recognize that this is an additional duty for most stakeholders. Ensuring that the requirements are simple and are a match for the stakeholders' capabilities is equally important. The plan should establish routine reporting requirements with standardized formats and timelines that are repeatable for any project, regardless of COCOM ownership or whether the solution is materiel- or training-related. Finally, the reporting requirements should avoid redundancy and unnecessary data collection.

Improve coordination with key agencies. The final insight of track 1, improving coordination, should ensure early input into 1206 projects from all stakeholders, including DoS. The plan should ensure that stakeholders are aware of the guidance, their roles and responsibilities, and their reporting requirements regarding the 1206 Program generally and the assessment process specifically. Clear communication early on will help ensure that the assessment process is effective in collecting and producing quality data, getting those data to the appropriate office, and conducting the assessment in a timely, effective, and unbiased way. Improving coordination also applies to the relationship between DoD and DoS and key congressional committees, where there is some concern about the need to establish a systematic assessment process for the 1206 Program. Keeping key committee members informed of progress vis-à-vis 1206 Program and project assessment plans and results will be critical to maintaining support for the program in Congress.

Track 2: Long-Term Actions

Track 2 comprises a set of more costly and time-consuming actions that could be implemented in the medium to long term to ensure that a comprehensive assessment process is in place. It expands on actions taken in track 1, outlines additional actions to enable more cost-effective and efficient management of the 1206 Program, and leverages technologies to streamline data collection. Implementation of both tracks would require wide dissemination of guidance to all potential stakeholders, including DSCA, the COCOMs, and the services. OUSD(P) should seek the input of external stakeholders, such as DoS and congressional staffs, throughout the process. As part of the rollout of the plan, OUSD(P) should also consider hosting a one-day conference to introduce the plan and lead discussions on its implementation in the coming fiscal year.

Set measurable objectives that explicitly connect to broader U.S. government, theater, regional, and 1206 Program goals. Track 1 suggests that the initial guidance document should identify the sources of program objectives as well as those stakeholders responsible for setting them at the project and activity levels. However, developing measurable objectives across the 1206 Program, i.e., between projects and within the program as a whole, is a much more challenging task. To begin with, objectives should explicitly connect the projects to counterterrorism or stability operations goals or to building partner capacity goals or both. Moreover, program managers must ensure that program and project objectives harmonize with congressional intent for the 1206 Program.

Such a task will require a repeatable process for setting measurable objectives, especially longer-term objectives that extend beyond the one-year focus of the program. Personnel rotation and policy shifts can further complicate such an effort. In designing the process, OUSD(P) should consider drawing from other, preexisting processes, such as the USPACOM model discussed in Chapter Three, that might be suitable for adaptation.

Refine roles for data collection and analysis based on track 1 lessons. Drawing on the lessons from implementing track 1, OUSD(P) should find it possible to refine the assessment roles for data collection, assessment, and integration. Processes put into place should be consistent yet flexible enough to absorb the lessons and evolve into an improved set of tools for assessing the 1206 Program.

Implement an automated system for data collection and assessment. Routine data collection is essential to the proper functioning of an assessment program, but with widely scattered data sources, personnel rotations, and limited training on assessment techniques, it can tail off over time. Efforts to simplify data collection, such as the employment of an automated data collection system, can help ensure the continued collection of essential data. Any automated tool should be "modular" and include the results of multiple projects over time. Such capability will facilitate cost-effectiveness, design and theory, and other levels of assessment.

Data collection tools can range from required email reports to more sophisticated, standalone systems. OUSD(P) or DSCA should consider identifying potential off-the-shelf automated tools or consulting with internal sources, such as the Office of the Deputy Assistant Secretary of Defense for Partnership Strategy and Stability Operations, to develop such an automated tool. Planning for the implementation of such a tool should include a pilot test, or tests, to compare candidate systems.

Rollout of the Assessment Implementation Plan

This section provides a time-phased rollout process, addressing development and execution of the implementation plan. The first phase focuses on the development of the plan, the second addresses coordination, and the third considers steps necessary for the plan's execution.

Development (1–6 months). Development of the implementation plan and formal guidance should begin in OUSD(P) with the process of consolidating existing guidance. Reviewing prior informal guidance to stakeholders, applicable policies, and regulations that cover related processes (such as FMS) is an essential first step in preparing the formal guidance. As a major part of the implementation plan, OUSD(P) should identify the data necessary for conducting strategic-level assessments for the 1206 Program (i.e., at the cost-effectiveness level).

The next step in this phase is defining processes for setting measureable objectives and data collection and making the initial assignment of roles and responsibilities for OUSD(P), DSCA, the COCOMs, and the services. Finally, OUSD(P) should begin exploring options for developing an automated data collection tool, possibly with the support of the Office of the Deputy Assistant Secretary of Defense for Partnership Strategy and Stability Operations.

Coordination (6–12 months). With the initial draft of the formal guidance, the first step in the coordination phase could be a strategic-level seminar that includes OUSD(P); DSCA; DoS; COCOM J4 (logistics), J5 (strategic plans and policy), and J8 (force structure, resources, and assessment); and the services at GS-15/colonel level. The main goals of this seminar would be to socialize the assessment concept, coordinate guidance, and solicit feedback. The seminar would complement the execution-level meetings that DSCA is currently hosting but would be at a higher level.

Following the initial coordination seminar, OUSD(P) should share the contents of the formal guidance and the assessment implementation plan with DoS and key congressional committees. Finally, with input from stakeholders from all levels, it will be possible to finalize assigned stakeholder roles and responsibilities before circulating the formal guidance for comment and approval.

Execution (12 months or more). After certain elements of the assessment implementation plan are rolled out in the first and second phases, the plan should be fully executed by the beginning of the third phase. This includes the publication of formal guidance to implement the recommendations presented in this chapter, as well as the development and deployment of the automated data collection and reporting tool.

Conclusion

We designed the recommendations in this chapter to help OUSD(P) establish a comprehensive assessment framework for the 1206 Program. Recognizing that an incremental approach will best satisfy OUSD(P)'s need to put an assessment framework into place as soon as possible, the assessment implementation plan posits a two-track approach that focuses on near-term actions that can be taken quickly and with limited costs. The longer-term actions in track 2 will help shore up track 1's limited scope, ensuring that the 1206 Program has a comprehensive and robust assessment program in place. Finally, the rollout plan offers advice on sequencing the activities in a way that will garner broad-based support across the 1206 Program community.

The Assessment Survey

This appendix presents the online survey that was administered to 1206 Program stakeholders in August 2010. The survey results and related analysis are presented in Chapter Four.

Part I. Your Information

Please provide the information requested below. This information will allow us to fully understand your organization's role as a stakeholder in the Section 1206 Global Train and Equip Program.

THIS STUDY: This study is being conducted within the International Security and Defense Policy Center of the RAND National Defense Research Institute, a federally funded research and development center sponsored by the Office of the Secretary of Defense, the Joint Staff, the Unified Combatant Commands, the Navy, the Marine Corps, the defense agencies, and the defense Intelligence Community. The sponsor of this study is the Office of the Deputy Assistant Secretary of Defense for Special Operations and Combating Terrorism in OASD(SO/LIC&IC)

PURPOSE: The purpose of this survey is to obtain data from 1206 Program stakeholders about the ability of their offices/units/activities to collect information concerning the 1206 Program and events that might support the assessment of the 1206 Program and related activities and events.

ROUTINE USES: This information will be used as inputs to an analysis of the Department of Defense's preparedness to conduct assessments of its 1206 Program. The results will help senior officials determine what additional steps, if any, the service should take in order to be able to perform the assessments required by the Guidance for the Employment of the Force (GEF) and by law pursuant to Section 1237 of the FY10 National Defense Authorization Act (NDAA).

DISCLOSURE: Participation is voluntary. No adverse action of any kind may be taken against any individual who elects not to participate in any portion of the survey. Personal identifying information will not be used in any reports—only aggregate data will be reported.

1. Please enter your rank or grade:

2. Are you a contractor?
    O Yes
    O No

3. Please enter your organization and office symbol:

4. Please enter your position and title:

Part II. Your Involvement in Specific Section 1206 Global Train and Equip Projects

Each year, multiple security cooperation projects are conducted under the Section 1206 Global Train and Equip Program (Section 1206). Some stakeholders are engaged in the overall management of the **program**, while others are engaged only in **specific projects**.

Were you involved in an aspect of the **overall management of the program**? If yes, you will proceed to Part III.

    O Yes
    O No

Were you involved **only with specific projects** (for example, you are, or have been, involved with one or more projects in a given COCOM AOR)? If yes, please enter the following requested information for **ONE PROJECT ONLY** in which you have personally been involved. Then, repeat this survey for each project in which you were involved.

    O Yes
    O No

IMPORTANT: If you have been involved in more than one project, please identify the project that will be the basis for this survey in the questions provided below, then answer the remaining questions based on that one project. If you would like to provide answers based on additional projects, you will have the opportunity to complete this survey again. *(In other words, if you have a role in more than one project, you may complete a SEPARATE survey for each of the projects in which you have a role.)*

Enter the title of the project that will be the subject of the remainder of the questions in this survey (if unknown, briefly describe the project's objectives or purpose):

Enter the country (or countries) that the project focused on:

COCOM AOR:

Enter the fiscal year:

Part III. Instructions

1. The questions that follow may be answered by clicking "Yes" or "No." If you select "Yes" for a question, you may be asked to provide additional information that elaborates on your answer.

2. The following information regarding Section 1206 **stakeholder roles** may be referred to at any time while you are completing the survey:

   a. Within each program, stakeholders have various levels of responsibility for carrying out activities. Some stakeholders **implement processes**; in other words, program managers assign them specific tasks which they then must carry out. These tasks might include organizing an event or providing subject-matter expertise, establishing contracts or accounting for funds, or processing documentation required by instructions or other directives.

   b. Other stakeholders participate in the **design or development of processes**, carrying out such activities as developing lesson plans, contracts, or event agendas.

   c. Some stakeholders **make recommendations** to program managers about the size of, scope of, or need for the program or a specific activity.

   d. Still other stakeholders **make decisions** regarding the specific activities, the need for, or the scope of the program.

3. Please answer each of the questions below as they relate to your duties **with regard to the project** for which you are completing this survey. In particular, please be sure to respond to follow-on requests for specific information related to the roles, responsibilities, and functions you perform (e.g., events, activities, and types and sources of data).

4. Please be as complete as possible, avoiding any acronyms or abbreviations.

Part III.A. Process Implementation

5. Do you manage resources that are used in the implementation of the Section 1206 project?
   O Yes
   O Don't Know/Not Applicable
   O No

5a. If you answered "Yes," please list the resources you manage:
   O People
   O Funds
   O Facilities
   O Infrastructure
   O Other, please specify

6. Do you directly observe or participate in any of the specific events or activities executed using Section 1206 funds with partner nations?
   O Yes
   O Don't Know/Not Applicable
   O No

6a. If you answered "Yes," please list the events or activities you observe:
   O Conference, Subject-Matter Expert Exchange, or Roundtable Discussion
   O Contract Award
   O Contract Performance
   O Delivery of Equipment
   O Equipment Installation
   O Field Exercise
   O Provision of Supplies or Spares
   O Tabletop Exercise
   O Training
   O Upgrades, Maintenance, or Repairs to Equipment
   O Other, please specify

7. Do you collect data regarding the timeliness, accuracy, or appropriateness of the assistance provided to partner nation(s)?
   O Yes
   O Don't Know/Not Applicable
   O No

7a. If you answered "Yes," please describe the types of data you collect and the sources of the data:
   O After-Action Reports
   O Bills of Lading or Other Receipts for the Delivery of Goods
   O Contract Award
   O Contract Performance
   O Letter of Acceptance
   O Memoranda of Agreement

○ My Own Observations/Trip Report
○ Project Agreement/Arrangement Memos
○ Project Proposal
○ Quality Assurance Reports
○ Reports to Congress
○ Status, Update, IPR, or Similar Briefings
○ Training Quotas
○ Training Reports
○ Travel Orders
○ Visit Request
○ Other, please specify

8. Do you collect data regarding partner-nation representatives, such as attendees, participants, recipients, or numbers of individuals trained?
○ Yes
○ Don't Know/Not Applicable
○ No

8a. If you answered "Yes," please describe the types of data you collect and the sources of the data:
○ After-Action Reports
○ Discussion with Country Desk Officers
○ Discussion with Partner-Nation Representatives
○ Discussion with Country Team Members
○ Guest Lists
○ International Visit Request
○ Travel Orders or Invitational Travel Orders
○ Letter of Acceptance
○ Letter of Request
○ My Own Observations/Trip Report
○ Nomination Package
○ Quality Assurance Report
○ Status, Update, or IPR Briefing
○ Training Quotas
○ Training Report
○ Vetting Processes
○ Visit Request
○ Other, please specify

9. Do you collect data regarding participant views or observations, such as exit surveys?
○ Yes
○ Don't Know/Not Applicable
○ No

9a. If you answered "Yes," please describe the types of data you collect and the sources of the data:
- O After-Action Reports
- O Informal Discussions
- O Meeting Minutes/Summary
- O My Own Observations/Trip Report
- O Progress Report
- O Project Final Report
- O Project Quarterly Report
- O Quality Assurance Report
- O Test and Disposition Report
- O Training Report
- O Other, please specify

10. Do you collect data regarding capabilities assessments?
- O Yes
- O Don't Know/Not Applicable
- O No

10a. If you answered "Yes," please describe the sources of the data you collect:
- O Country Desk Officers
- O Discussion with Partner-Nation Representatives
- O Discussions with Country Team Members
- O Exchange Agreement
- O Intelligence Sources
- O International Agreements
- O Memorandum of Agreement
- O Memorandum of Understanding
- O My Own Observations/Trip Report
- O Participant Entry or Exit Testing
- O Site Survey Reports
- O U.S. Military Trainers
- O Other, please specify

11. Do you collect data regarding the effect of the 1206 project on relevant partner capabilities?
- O Yes
- O Don't Know/Not Applicable
- O No

11a. If you answered "Yes," please describe the types of data you collect and the sources of the data:
- O After-Action Reports
- O Annual Report
- O Certification to Congress
- O End-of-Tour Report
- O Interim Tour Report

O Meeting Minutes/Summary
O My Own Observations/Trip Report
O Progress Report
O Project Quarterly Report
O Quality Assurance Report
O Quid Pro Quo Analysis
O Test and Disposition Report
O Training Report
O Other, please specify

12. Do you collect data regarding the funds expended?
O Yes
O Don't Know/Not Applicable
O No

12a. If you answered "Yes," please describe the types of data you collect and the sources of the data:
O Budget Allocation Memo
O Budget Projection
O Budget Request
O Loan Agreement
O My Own Observations/Trip Report
O Periodic Financial Report
O Quarterly Obligation Report
O Request for Fund Cite
O Travel Vouchers
O Other, please specify

13. Do you collect data regarding compliance with legal or regulatory requirements related to the project?
O Yes
O Don't Know/Not Applicable
O No

13a. If you answered "Yes," please describe the types of data you collect and the sources of the data:
O Releasability Requests
O Request for Human Rights Vetting
O FAA Section 505 Agreement
O Data Exchange Annex
O Delegation of Disclosure Authority Letter
O Extended Visit Authorization
O Information Exchange Agreement
O My Own Observations/Trip Report
O Request for Foreign Disclosure Authorization
O Security Plan
O Other, please specify

14. Do you collect data regarding program implementation that was not mentioned above?
- O Yes
- O Don't Know/Not Applicable
- O No

14a. If you answered "Yes," please describe the types of data you collect and the sources of the data:

15. Do you prepare reports that document specific activities or events (i.e., trip reports, after-action reports, surveys, etc.)?
- O Yes
- O Don't Know/Not Applicable
- O No

15a. If you answered "Yes," please indicate which documents you prepare:
- O Program Proposal
- O Requirements of Proposal Prioritization Document
- O FAA Section 505 Agreement
- O Releasability Request
- O Human Rights Vetting Request
- O Embassy Concurrent Cable
- O After-Action Report
- O Annual Report
- O Financial Reports
- O Monthly Report
- O My Own Observations/Trip Report
- O Programmatic Review
- O Progress Report
- O Project Final Report
- O Quality Assurance Report
- O Quarterly Obligation Report
- O Report to Congress
- O Status, Update, or IPR Report
- O Test and Disposition Report
- O Training Report
- O Other, please specify

15b. If you answered "Yes," please describe in greater detail, if necessary, and please indicate which offices and organizations review the indicated documents:

Part III.B. Process Design and Development

16. Do you design specific events or activities for this Section 1206 project? (See below for examples of events and activities.)
    - O Yes
    - O Don't Know/Not Applicable
    - O No

16a. If you answered "Yes," please list the events or activities that you design:
    - O Acquisition of Equipment, Supplies, or Spares
    - O Meeting or Conference Agenda
    - O Actual Section 1206 Program Proposal
    - O Background Material
    - O Briefings
    - O Requirements or Proposal Prioritization Document
    - O Budget Allocation Memo
    - O Budget Projection
    - O Budget Request
    - O Site Survey
    - O Contract Preparation
    - O Lesson Plans or Other Training Material
    - O Letter of Request/Letter of Acceptance
    - O Master Data Agreement
    - O Master Information Agreement
    - O Project Proposal
    - O Proposal Development
    - O Request for Disclosure Authorization
    - O Request for Fund Cite
    - O Security Plan
    - O Visit Request
    - O Other, please specify

17. Do you develop documents such as instructions or other directives that guide or govern the conduct of activities or events within the project? If so, what are these documents?
    - O Yes
    - O Don't Know/Not Applicable
    - O No

17a. If you answered "Yes," please list these documents:
    - O Proposal Standard Template
    - O Annual Guidance
    - O Program DoDI
    - O Briefings
    - O Cables
    - O Contracts
    - O Data Exchange Annex

O Directives
O Emails
O Guidance Memoranda
O Information Exchange Agreement
O Instructions
O International Agreement
O International Program Directive
O Master Data Agreement
O Master Information Agreement
O Memorandum of Agreement
O Memorandum of Understanding
O Operating Procedures
O Project Agreement/Arrangement
O Project Nomination Form
O Project Proposal
O Quality Assurance Plans
O Security Plan
O Visit Request
O Other, please specify

18. Are the design and development of activities or events for your project governed by any DoD instructions, manuals, or other directives?
O Yes
O Don't Know/Not Applicable
O No

18a. If you answered "Yes," please list these documents:

19. Are the design and development of activities or events for your project governed by any non-DoD instructions, manuals, or other directives?
O Yes
O Don't know/Not Applicable
O No

19a. If you answered "Yes," please list these documents:

20. Are there informal documents (e.g., continuity binders) that you refer to in the design and development of the events or activities for your project?

    O Yes

    O Don't Know/Not Applicable

    O No

20a. If you answered "Yes," please list these documents:

21. Do you collect data regarding the cost of the overall project or the cost of a unit of output (i.e., one graduate, one event, etc.)?

    O Yes

    O Don't Know/Not Applicable

    O No

21a. If you answered "Yes," please describe these data, and please indicate which offices or organizations review them:

    O Periodic Financial Report

    O Travel Vouchers

    O Budget Allocation Memo

    O Budget Projection

    O Budget Request

    O Quarterly Obligation Report

    O 319 Funds Transfer

    O Request for Fund Cite

    O Travel Orders

    O Other, please specify

21b. If you answered "Yes," please describe in greater detail, if necessary, and please indicate which offices or organizations review the indicated documents:

Part III.C. Program Recommendations

22. Do you make recommendations regarding the overall need for the project?
    O Yes
    O Don't Know/Not Applicable
    O No

22a. If you answered "Yes," please list the stakeholder(s) (i.e., office or organization) that receive(s) your recommendations:

23. Do you make recommendations regarding the need to increase or reduce participation in the project?
    O Yes
    O Don't Know/Not Applicable
    O No

23a. If you answered "Yes," please list the stakeholder(s) (i.e., office or organization) that receive(s) your recommendations:

24. Do you make recommendations regarding which countries participate in the program?
    O Yes
    O Don't Know/Not Applicable
    O No

24a. If you answered "Yes," please list the stakeholder(s) (i.e., office or organization) that receive(s) your recommendations:

25. Do you gather data that reflect how well a specific event or activity met its objectives?
    O Yes
    O Don't Know/Not Applicable
    O No

25a. If you answered "Yes," please describe the type of data:
    O After-Action Reports
    O Annual Report
    O Certification to Congress
    O Meeting Minutes/Summary

O Monthly Report
O My Own Observations/Trip Report
O Progress Report
O Project Final Report
O Project Quarterly Report
O Quality Assurance Report
O Quarterly Obligation Report
O Status, Update, or IPR Briefings
O Test and Disposition Report
O Training Report
O Other, please specify

26. Do you advocate for funds used to implement the project?
O Yes
O Don't Know/Not Applicable
O No

26a. If you answered "Yes," please describe the process(es) you use:

Part III.D. Program Decisions

27. Do you contribute to the determination of the overall need for specific projects?
    O Yes
    O Don't Know/Not Applicable
    O No

27a. If you answered "Yes," please list the process(es) you use, or participate in, to make this determination:

28. Do you set the objectives for the specific projects?
    O Yes
    O Don't Know/Not Applicable
    O No

28a. If you answered "Yes," where are the objectives documented?

29. Do you set the objectives for specific events or activities within specific projects?
    O Yes
    O Don't Know/Not Applicable
    O No

29a. If you answered "Yes," where are the objectives documented?

30. Do you have access to information regarding other DoD security cooperation programs, such as their objectives, cost, benefits, and the priorities attached to each?
    O Yes
    O Don't Know/Not Applicable
    O No

30a. If you answered "Yes," what are your sources for this information?

31. Do you have access to information regarding other DoD programs (not security cooperation) and the priority attached to each?

   o Yes

   o Don't Know/Not Applicable

   o No

31a. If you answered "Yes," what are your sources for this information?

32. Do you have access to information regarding other DoD programs (not security cooperation) and their objectives, cost, and benefits?

   o Yes

   o Don't Know/Not Applicable

   o No

32a. If you answered "Yes," what are your sources for this information?

Part III.E. Program Assessment Skills

33. Do you believe that you, or personnel assigned to your position in the future, have/will have the skills to conduct appropriate security cooperation assessments (e.g., regarding the need for a program, program design, program compliance with policy, program outcomes, and program cost-effectiveness)?
    - O Yes
    - O Don't Know/Not Applicable
    - O No

34. If no, do you believe that you, or personnel assigned to your position in the future, would be prepared to conduct assessments if you had an appropriate checklist and set of instructions?
    - O Yes
    - O Don't Know/Not Applicable
    - O No

35. If no, do you believe that completion of a short course on conducting assessments (via classroom or online instruction) would be adequate preparation for someone in your position?
    - O Yes
    - O Don't Know/Not Applicable
    - O No

36. Please share with us any additional information you believe is pertinent to our inquiry or any comments you have about the instrument or our research:

IMPORTANT: If you have been involved in more than one project, **please complete a separate survey for each project**. When you click the **Done** button below, the information for this survey will be submitted and you will be returned to the original survey web page. At this point, you may click on the survey link to open a new survey, where you may answer questions based on an additional project in which you were involved.

Thank you for your participation in this information gathering exercise.

Focused Discussions

This appendix presents a list of the affiliations of participants in our focused discussions.

U.S. Congress
   House Armed Services Committee
   House Foreign Affairs Committee
   Senate Appropriations Committee, Defense Subcommittee
   Senate Armed Services Committee

U.S. Department of Defense
   Defense Security Cooperation Agency
   Joint Staff
   Navy International Programs Office
   Office of the Secretary of the Air Force for International Affairs
   Office of the Under Secretary of Defense for Policy
   U.S. Africa Command
   U.S. Army Security Assistance Command
   U.S. Central Command
   U.S. European Command
   U.S. Northern Command
   U.S. Pacific Command
   U.S. Southern Command
   U.S. Special Operations Command

U.S. Department of State
   Bureau of Political-Military Affairs

Bibliography

Air Force Instruction 16-101, International Affairs and Security Assistance Management, February 15, 2011.

Defense Security Cooperation Agency, *Security Assistance Management Manual*, Washington, D.C., DoD 5105.38M, October 3, 2003.

———, "Guidance for Development of FY09 Section 1206 Programs," memorandum, February 3, 2009.

Marquis, Jefferson P., Richard E. Darilek, Jasen J. Castillo, Cathryn Quantic Thurston, Anny Wong, Cynthia Huger, Andrea Mejia, Jennifer D. P. Moroney, Brian Nichiporuk, and Brett Steele, *Assessing the Value of U.S. Army International Activities*, Santa Monica, Calif.: RAND Corporation, MG-329-A, 2006. As of December 30, 2010:
http://www.rand.org/pubs/monographs/MG329.html

Marquis, Jefferson P., Joe Hogler, Jennifer D. P. Moroney, Michael J. Neumann, Christopher Paul, John E. Peters, Gregory F. Treverton, and Anny Wong, *Adding Value to Air Force Management Through Building Partnerships Assessment*, Santa Monica, Calif.: RAND Corporation, TR-907-AF, 2010. As of December 30, 2010:
http://www.rand.org/pubs/technical_reports/TR907.html

Marquis, Jefferson P., Jennifer D. P. Moroney, Justin Beck, Derek Eaton, Scott Hiromoto, David R. Howell, Janet Lewis, Charlotte Lynch, Michael J. Neumann, and Cathryn Quantic Thurston, *Developing an Army Strategy for Building Partner Capacity for Stability Operations*, Santa Monica, Calif.: RAND Corporation, MG-942-A, 2010. As of December 30, 2010:
http://www.rand.org/pubs/monographs/MG942.html

Moroney, Jennifer D. P., and Joe Hogler, with Benjamin Bahney, Kim Cragin, David R. Howell, Charlotte Lynch, and S. Rebecca Zimmerman, *Building Partner Capacity to Combat Weapons of Mass Destruction*, Santa Monica, Calif.: RAND Corporation, MG-783-DTRA, 2009. As of December 30, 2010:
http://www.rand.org/pubs/monographs/MG783.html

Moroney, Jennifer D. P., Joe Hogler, Jefferson P. Marquis, Christopher Paul, John E. Peters, and Beth Grill, *Developing an Assessment Framework for U.S. Air Force Building Partnerships Programs*, Santa Monica, Calif.: RAND Corporation, MG-868-AF, 2010. As of December 30, 2010:
http://www.rand.org/pubs/monographs/MG868.html

Moroney, Jennifer D. P., Jefferson P. Marquis, Cathryn Quantic Thurston, and Gregory F. Treverton, *A Framework to Assess Programs for Building Partnerships*, Santa Monica, Calif.: RAND Corporation, MG-863-OSD, 2009. As of December 30, 2010:
http://www.rand.org/pubs/monographs/MG863.html

Paul, Christopher, Harry J. Thie, Elaine Reardon, Deanna Weber Prine, and Laurence Smallman, *Implementing and Evaluating an Innovative Approach to Simulation Training Acquisitions*, Santa Monica, Calif.: RAND Corporation, MG-442-OSD, 2006. As of December 30, 2010:
http://www.rand.org/pubs/monographs/MG442.html

Rossi, Peter H., Mark W. Lipsey, and Howard E. Freeman, *Evaluation: A Systematic Approach*, 7th ed., Thousand Oaks, Calif.: Sage Publications, 2004.

Schonlau, Matthias, Ronald D. Fricker, and Marc N. Elliott, *Conducting Research Surveys via E-Mail and the Web*, Santa Monica, Calif.: RAND Corporation, MR-1480-RC, 2002. As of December 30, 2010:
http://www.rand.org/pubs/monograph_reports/MR1480.html

U.S. Congress, National Defense Authorization Act for Fiscal Year 2010, H.R. 2647, Sec. 1206, January 6, 2009. As of December 30, 2010:
http://www.gpo.gov/fdsys/pkg/BILLS-111hr2647enr/pdf/BILLS-111hr2647enr.pdf

U.S. Department of Defense and U.S. Department of State, Offices of the Inspectors General, *Interagency Evaluation of the Section 1206 Global Train and Equip Program*, Washington, D.C., August 31, 2009. As of December 30, 2010:
http://oig.state.gov/documents/organization/129491.pdf

U.S. Government Accountability Office, *International Security: DoD and State Need to Improve Sustainment Planning and Monitoring and Evaluation for Section 1206 and 1207 Assistance Programs*, Washington, D.C., GAO-10-431, April 15, 2010. As of December 30, 2010:
http://www.gao.gov/new.items/d10431.pdf